BASIC BIBLE
DOCTRINES

OF THE
CHRISTIAN FAITH

UNDERSTANDING THE CREATION ACCOUNT

Edward D. Andrews

GENESIS 1-4

UNDERSTANDING THE CREATION ACCOUNT

Basic Bible Doctrines of the Christian Faith

Edward D. Andrews

Christian Publishing House

Cambridge, Ohio

Christian Publishing House

Professional Christian Publishing of the Good News

UNDERSTANDING THE CREATION ACCOUNT: Basic Bible Doctrines of the Christian Faith

ISBN-13: 978-0692657072

ISBN-10: 069265707X

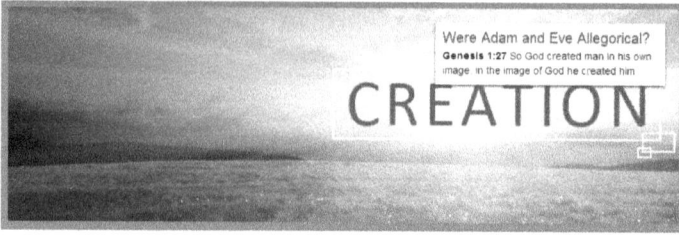

Were Adam and Eve Allegorical?

Genesis 1:27 So God created man in his own image, in the image of God he created him

CREATION

Table of Content

CHAPTER 1 Adam and Eve Before Sinning and Rebelling

THE SIXTH CREATION DAY: Historical Written Record Narrative

Genesis 1:27-31 Updated American Standard Version (ASV)

27 So God created man in his own image,
in the image of God he created him;
male and female he created them.

28 And God blessed them. And God said to them, "Be fruitful and multiply and fill the earth and subdue it, and have dominion over the fish of the sea and over the birds of the heavens and over every living thing that moves on the earth." **29** And God said, "Behold, I have given you every plant yielding seed that is on the face of all the earth, and every tree with seed in its fruit. You shall have them for food. **30** And to every beast of the earth and to every bird of the heavens and to everything that creeps on the earth, everything that has the breath of life, I have given every green plant for food." And it was so. **31** And God saw everything that he had made, and behold, it was very good. And there was evening and there was morning, the sixth day.

God blessed Adam and Eve and commanded them to "be fruitful and multiply and fill the earth and subdue it. There are three references to procreating, "be fruitful," "multiply," and "fill the earth." If Adam and Eve were just allegorical characters that represented early humanity, why the command to do what they were clearly already doing, to procreate and fill the earth?

FORBIDDEN TREE OF KNOWLEDGE: Historical Written Record Narrative

Genesis 2:15-17 Updated American Standard Version American Standard Version (ASV)

15 And Jehovah God took the man and set him in the garden of Eden to cultivate it and to keep it. **16** And Jehovah God commanded the man, saying, "From every tree of the garden you may freely eat, **17** but from the tree of the knowledge of good and evil you shall not eat,[1] for in the day that you eat from it you shall surely die."[2]

The Hebrew אָדָם ('adam) occurs 556 times in **524** verses in the Hebrew concordance of the NASB.

Outline of Biblical Usage

- man, mankind

- man, a human being

- man, mankind (much more frequently intended sense in OT)

- Adam, first man

- city in Jordan Valley

Every reference to a man in Genesis 1-4 is to one man, Adam, not to mankind, i.e., the context and the personal pronouns that refer back to him. God did not set early humanity in the Garden of Eden to cultivate it, but rather he did so with a real historical person, Adam.[3]

The Bible is silent as to the type of tree. However, the idea of the tree being symbolic is correct. The tree was a literal tree with literal fruit, but the fruit did not really have any special powers. The fruit had no intrinsic power to give knowledge, as was evidenced after their eating from it. It did symbolize God's right of sovereignty, His right to set a standard of what is good and bad. To eat from the tree would have been a rejection of that sovereignty, a rebellion that said that could set their own standard of good and bad, independence from their creator. This was a simple test, for a couple that was to serve as the father and mother of a perfect human race. A footnote on Genesis 2:17, in The Jerusalem Bible (1966):

---

[1] Lit *eat from it*

[2] Lit., *dying you* [singular] *shall die.* Heb., moth tamuth; the first reference to death in the Scriptures

[3] Adam was made the gardener in Eden. This was an easy and pleasant assignment because it was a source of great joy. It was the only work he was given to do—if such an occupation can even be called "work" in a sweatless, weedless, curse-free environment. His only responsibility was to make sure that the trees and plants had appropriate care. He was a guardian and steward of its wonders and resources.–MacArthur, John (2005-05-09). *The MacArthur Bible Commentary* (Kindle Locations 2003-2006). Thomas Nelson. Kindle Edition.

This knowledge is a privilege which God reserves to himself and which man, by sinning, is to lay hands on, 3:5, 22. Hence it does not mean omniscience, which fallen man does not possess; nor is it moral discrimination, for unfallen man already had it and God could not refuse it to a rational being. It is the power of deciding for himself what is good and what is evil and of acting accordingly, a claim to complete moral independence by which man refuses to recognize his status as a created being. The first sin was an attack on God's sovereignty, a sin of pride.

THE CREATION OF EVE: Historical Written Record Narrative

Genesis 2:18-24 Updated American Standard Version (UASV)

18 Then Jehovah God said, "It is not good for the man to be alone; I will make him a helper for him.[4] **19** And out of the ground Jehovah God formed every beast of the field, and every bird of the heavens; and brought them to the man to see what he would call them; and whatsoever the man called every living soul, that was its name. **20** And the man gave names to all cattle, and to the birds of the heavens, and to every beast of the field; but for man there was found no helper as a counterpart of him. **21** So Jehovah God caused a deep sleep to fall upon the man, and he slept; then he took one of his ribs and closed up the flesh at that place. **22** and the rib that Jehovah God had taken from the man he made into a woman and brought her to the man.

23 Then the man said,

"This at last is bone of my bones
and flesh of my flesh;
she shall be called Woman,
because she was taken out of Man."

24 Therefore a man shall leave his father and his mother and be joined to his wife, and they shall be as one flesh. **25** And the man and his wife were both naked and were not ashamed.

Why the concern for loneliness if it were an allegorical account of early mankind? In addition, Adam was assigned the task of naming the

---

[4] Lit "as his opposite;" *counterpart or complement*, something that completes or perfects him

different kinds of animals. This is not a simple task of just picking a name randomly. In the ancient culture, names carried even more meaning than in our modern Western culture. Names were chosen to be descriptive, to reflect something about the person, animal, or thing. From the descriptive forms of the names Adam chose, it is obvious that it took some time, for the account literally reads "whatever the man called *every living creature, that was its name.*"[5] (Genesis 2:19) For example, the Hebrew word for the "ass" refers to the usually reddened color. The Hebrew word for stork is the feminine form of the word meaning "loyal one."[6] This name is certainly a perfect fit, as the stork is known for the loving care it gives its young, and the loyalty of staying with its mate for life.

---

[5] Walter A. Elwell and Barry J Beitzel, *Baker Encyclopedia of the Bible* (Grand Rapids, Mich.: Baker Book House, 1988), S. 93.

[6] Walter A. Elwell and Barry J Beitzel, *Baker Encyclopedia of the Bible* (Grand Rapids, Mich.: Baker Book House, 1988), S. 93.

Review Questions

- How does the command to procreate add to the historicity of Adam and Eve?

- How does reference to man in Genesis chapters 1-4 suggest a real, historical person?

- What can be said about the tree of knowledge?

- How do loneliness and the naming of animals evidence that Adam, Eve, and the Garden of Eden is a real historical account?

CHAPTER 2 Adam Rebelled Choosing Eve Over His Creator

THE TEMPTATION AND THE FALL OF ADAM: Historical Written Record Narrative

Genesis 3:1-7 Updated American Standard Version (UASV)

3 Now the serpent was more crafty than any beast of the field which Jehovah God had made. And he said to the woman, "Did God actually say, 'You[7] shall not eat of any tree in the garden'?" **2** And the woman said to the serpent, "From the fruit of the trees of the garden we may eat, **3** but from the tree that is in the midst of the garden, God said, 'You shall not eat from it, nor shall you touch it, lest you die'." **4** And the serpent said to the woman, "You shall not surely die. **5** For God knows that when you eat of it your eyes will be opened, and you will be like God, knowing good and evil." knowing good and evil.

6 So when the woman saw that the tree was good for food, and that it was a delight to the eyes, and that the tree was to be desirable to make one wise, and she took of its fruit and ate, then she also gave some to her husband when with her, and he ate. **7** Then the eyes of both of them were opened, and they knew that they were naked; and they sewed fig leaves together and made themselves loin coverings.

Here again we have a historical record that is a narrative of two real people. Are we to assume that all former women allegorically represent by Eve, handed all former men, represented by Adam, a piece of fruit and they all ate?

---

[7] In Hebrew *you* is plural in verses 1–5

Review Questions

- Explain how Genesis 3:1-7 is a historical narrative.

CHAPTER 3 Adam and Eve Outside the Garden of Eden

THE COST OF SIN: Historical Written Record Narrative

Genesis 3:8-24 Updated American Standard Version (UASV)

The Costs of Sin

8 Then they heard the sound[8] of Jehovah God walking in the garden at the wind[9] of the day, and the man and his wife hid themselves from the presence of Jehovah God among the trees of the garden. **9** Then Jehovah God called to the man, and said to him, "Where are you?" **10** And he said, "I heard the sound of you in the garden, and I was afraid, because I was naked, and I hid myself." **11** And he said, "Who told you that you were naked? Have you eaten from the tree of which I commanded you not to eat?" **12** The man said, "The woman whom you gave to be with me, she gave me from the tree, and I ate." **13** Then Jehovah God said to the woman, "What is this you have done?" And the woman said, "The serpent deceived me, and I ate."

14 Jehovah God said to the serpent,

"Because you have done this,
    cursed are you above all livestock
    and above all beasts of the field;
on your belly you shall go,
    and dust you shall eat
    all the days of your life.
15 And I will put enmity between you and the woman,
    and between your seed and her seed;
he shall bruise your head,
    and you shall bruise his heel."

16 To the woman he said,

"I will surely multiply your pain in childbearing;
    in pain you shall bring forth children.
Your desire shall be for your husband,
    and he shall rule over you."

---

[8] Lit *the voice*

[9] Or in the *cool* of the day

17 And to Adam he said,

"Because you have listened to the voice of your wife
  and have eaten of the tree
of which I commanded you,
  'You shall not eat of it,'
cursed is the ground because of you;
  in toil you shall eat of it all the days of your life;
18 Both thorns and thistles it shall bring forth for you;
  and you shall eat the plants of the field.
19 By the sweat of your face
  you shall eat bread,
till you return to the ground,
  for out of it you were taken;
for you are dust,
  and to dust you shall return."

20 Now the man called his wife's name Eve, because she was the mother of all living. **21** And Jehovah God made for Adam and for his wife garments of skins and clothed them. **22** Then Jehovah God said, "Behold, the man has become like one of us in knowing good and evil. Now, lest he reach out his hand and take also of the tree of life and eat, and live forever—" **23** therefore the Lord God sent him out from the garden of Eden, to cultivate the ground from which he was taken. **24** So he drove the man out, and at the east of the garden of Eden he placed the cherubim and a flaming sword that turned every way to guard the way to the tree of life.

We see a historical account of two persons being punished for their rebellion. We see in verse 20 that a real Eve would become the mother of all living. How is that possible if she is allegorical of early humans?

Review Questions

- Explain how Genesis 3:8-24 is a historical narrative.

CHAPTER 4 Were Adam and Eve Allegorical or Historical Persons?

Critical Scholars either consider Adam and Eve as a myth or symbolic persons, representing humankind. The evidence from the Bible, on the other hand is that they are real historical persons. Before looking at the biblical evidence, let us note that Hebrew manuscripts are archaeological evidence that give us the historicity of humanity. The oldest manuscripts date to the 3rd century BC. In addition, Greek New Testament manuscripts give us how Jewish Christians from the first century, as well as the Son of God views the Hebrew Old Testament and the historicity of Adam and Eve, and these NT MSS are archaeological evidence, dating as early as the second century AD.

Scriptural Evidence

(1) Genesis 1-2 is a historical narrative that expounds on Adam and Eve's creation and events within their lives. **(2)** They are recorded as giving birth to children, as do the others mentioned in the early genealogies. (Gen 4:1, 25; 5:1) **(3)** The Hebrew word toledoth, often translated "generations," should be translated "history" at Genesis 2:4; 5:1; 6:9; 10:1; 11:10; as well as five other places in Genesis. Regardless, it shows that toledoth is used all throughout Genesis, in speaking of descendants of so-and-so, and has the same meaning in its use with Adam and Eve at Genesis 5:1. **(4)** If we look at the chronologies throughout the Old Testament, Adam starts the list. (1 Ch 1:1) **(5)** All early humankind did not father Seth. No, Adam fathered him at the specific age of 130 years. (Gen 5:3) **(6)** Luke places Adam at the start of human history. (Lu 3:38) **(7)** Jesus viewed Adam and Eve as real historical persons. (Matt 19:24-25) **(8)** The inheritance of sin and death came from a literal Adam. (Rom 5:12-14) **(9)** Jesus is contrasted with Adam, which means if we deny Adam as a historical person, we deny Jesus Christ and his sacrifice as well. (1 Cor. 15:45-47) **(10)** Again, Paul comes to the stage as a witness, when he informs us that Adam was created first and then Eve. (1 Tim 2:13-14) **(11)** Was Enoch the seventh in line from all early humankind? (Jude14) Reasonably, humankind had to of started from just two people at some time. The fact is that the Bible, as a reliable book and archaeological evidence of human history, gives us those two people, Adam and Eve.

Has Science Now Caught Up With the Fact That All of Us Descended from the Same Original Parents?

Dr. Purdom explains:

The genetic evidence is consistent with human DNA being "young" and the human race beginning with a very small starting population (the Bible tells us the starting population was two people!).

The International HapMap project endeavors to study a select group of DNA similarities and differences between humans known as single nucleotide polymorphisms (SNPs).[10] The SNPs are believed to be representative of the genome (total human DNA) such that what is true for them would be true for the whole genome. These studies and others have shown that the difference in DNA between any two humans is amazingly low . . . only 0.1 percent.[11]

Reflecting on this very low percentage, some scientists posited, "This proportion is low compared with those of many other species, from fruit flies to chimpanzees, reflecting the recent origins of our species from a small founding population" (emphases mine).[12] They also stated, "[Certain genetic estimates] tell us that humans vary only slightly at the DNA level and that only a small proportion of this variation separates continental populations."[13]

These findings are consistent with the Bible's history that humans were created several thousand years ago; in other words, a short amount of time has passed, so there is little genetic variation.

The Bible Concurs

Acts 17:26 Updated American Standard Version (UASV)

and he [God] made from one man every nation of mankind to live on all the face of the earth, having determined their appointed times and the boundaries of their habitation,

---

[10] HapMap Homepage

[11] Lynn B. Jorde and Stephen P. Wooding, "Genetic Variation, Classification and 'Race'," Nature Genetics 36 (2004):S28–S33. Quoted in "Were Adam and Eve Real People," chapter 20 of How We Know the Bible is True volume 2, Green Forest, Arkansas: Master Books, 2012.

[12] IBID

[13] IBID

How does the Bible View Adam?

Jude 14 Updated American Standard Version (UASV)

[14] It was also about these men that Enoch, the seventh one in line from Adam,[14] prophesied, saying, "Behold, the Lord came with tens of thousands of his holy ones,

Note here that Jude makes a historical reference to Enoch being the seventh in line from Adam, not all, early mankind.

Luke 3:23-38 Updated American Standard Version (UASV)

[23] Jesus, when he began his ministry, was about thirty years of age, being the son (as was supposed) of Joseph, the son of Heli, . . . [31] son of David . . . [34] son of Abraham . . . [37] son of Adam."

Both David and Abraham are well-known historical persons, so why would Luke go through the genealogy of all many historical persons to get back to an allegorical person? Would not the Jews know if Adam were an allegorical person? Would it not make a genealogical list look quite silly, if one took it back to an allegorical person?

Genesis 5:3 Updated American Standard Version (UASV)

[3] When Adam had lived one hundred and thirty years, he became[15] the father of a son in his own likeness, according to his image, and named him Seth.

So, if Adam is allegorical, standing for early mankind, how do we reason that early mankind fathered Seth, specifically at 130 years of age?

Can the fact that we have a serpent speaking too Eve be used to argue for an allegorical story?

Genesis 3:1-4 Updated American Standard Version (UASV)

3 Now the serpent was more crafty than any beast of the field which Jehovah God had made. And he said to the woman, "Did God actually say, 'You[16] shall not eat of any tree in the

---

[14] Following the genealogy of Genesis 5:1–24; 1 Chronicles 1:1–3, Enoch was the seventh in the line of Adam. – MacArthur, John (2005-05-09). *The MacArthur Bible Commentary* (Kindle Locations 66202-66203). Thomas Nelson. Kindle Edition.

[15] Lit *begot*

[16] In Hebrew *you* is plural in verses 1–5

13

garden'?" **²** And the woman said to the serpent, "From the fruit of the trees of the garden we may eat, **³** but from the tree that is in the midst of the garden, God said, 'You shall not eat from it, nor shall you touch it, lest you die'." **⁴** And the **serpent said to the woman,** "You shall not surely die.

John 8:44 Updated American Standard Version (UASV)

⁴⁴ You are of your father the devil, and your will is to do your father's desires. That one was a manslayer from the beginning, and does not stand in the truth, because there is no truth in him. When he lies, he speaks out of his own character, for he is a liar and the father of lies.

We see here that Jesus, whose historicity is settled states unambiguously that Satan the Devil was the one behind the first lie in the Garden of Eden. Satan, a powerful angel (specifically a Cherub), spoke through the serpent, just as a ventriloquist can make his voice come through a dummy.

Revelation 12:9 Updated American Standard Version (UASV)

⁹ And the great dragon was thrown down, the serpent of old who is called the devil and Satan, who deceives the whole inhabited earth; he was thrown down to the earth, and his angels were thrown down with him.

If we say the first man Adam was allegorical, what does that mean for Jesus Christ, as we know he is not allegorical, making the contrast in Corinthians meaningless.

1 Corinthians 15:45, 47 Updated American Standard Version (UASV)

⁴⁵ So also it is written, "The first man, Adam, became a living soul." The last Adam became a life-giving spirit ... **⁴⁷** The first man is from the earth and made of dust; the second man is from heaven.

If we deny the historicity of Adam and his sin, a rebellion against God, it would mean the denial of the purpose of Jesus Christ's coming. Such a rejection is a motive for the anti-miracle Bible critics, activist atheists, who want such a rejection to be a repudiation of the Christian faith.

How did Jesus himself view the Genesis?

Matthew 19:4-5 Updated American Standard Version (UASV)

4 And he answered and said, "Have you not read that he who created them from the beginning made them male and female, **5** and said, 'For this reason a man shall leave his father and mother and be joined to his wife, and the two shall become one flesh'? [17]

Clearly, Jesus viewed the Genesis account to be factual and historical. If we look at the entire sixty-six books of the Bible, which covered 1,600 years of the history of the Israelite nation, written by forty+ men, all of which a belief in a historical Adam, it would seem that while we do not have archaeological evidence for the historicity of Adam, we have archaeological evidence that reference him as being a historical person that goes back to the third century B.C.E. up unto the sixteenth century C.E., i.e., well over 33,000 manuscripts. The irony is, those same secularists would not reject a real historical person, with far less evidence.

Sumeria

The first recorded name given in an actual writing system can be found on clay tablets dating from the Jemdet Nasr period in Sumeria between 3200 and 3101 BC.[18]

Image 1 Example of Jemdet Nasr cuneiform (Credit: Metropolitan Museum of Art

---

[17] 19:4 Quoted from Genesis 1:27; 5:2. Jesus' challenge to the Pharisees echoes the question raised by Malachi 2:15: "But did He not make them one?" (cf. verse 6). 19:5 Quoted from Genesis 2:24 (see note there).–MacArthur, John (2005-05-09). *The MacArthur Bible Commentary* (Kindle Locations 39971-39973). Thomas Nelson. Kindle Edition.

[18] Who Was the First Named Human? - The Huffington Post, http://www.huffingtonpost.com/dr-sten-odenwald/who-was-the-first-named-h_b_56798 (accessed February 17, 2016).

The tablets are not profound treatises on human thinking, but accounting ledgers for tallying up goods and possessions! Some of the first names are those of the slave owner Gal-Sal and his two slaves Enpap-x and Sukkalgir (3200-3100 BC). Another name is that of Turgunu Sanga (3100 BC) who seems to have been an accountant for the Turgunu family. There are many more names from this period but none that appear much before 3200 BC.[19]

What Is Recorded History?

Recorded history or written history is a historical narrative based on a written record or other documented communication. Recorded history can be contrasted with other narratives of the past such as mythological or oral traditions.

Historical Method

The historical method comprises the techniques and guidelines by which historians use primary sources and other evidence to research and then to write history. Primary sources are firsthand evidence of history (usually written, but sometimes captured in other mediums) made at the time of an event by a present person. Historians think of those sources as the closest to the origin of the information or idea under study.[20] These types of sources can provide researchers with, as Dalton and Charnigo put it, "direct, unmediated information about the object of study."[21]

---

[19] Who Was the First Named Human?

Who Was the First Named Human? - The Huffington Post, http://www.huffingtonpost.com/dr-sten-odenwald/who-was-the-first-named-h_b_56798 (accessed February 17, 2016).

[20] User Education Services. "Primary, Secondary and Tertiary Sources". University of Maryland Libraries. Retrieved 10 Jul 2013.

"Library Guides: Primary, secondary and tertiary sources"

[21] Dalton, Margaret Steig; Charnigo, Laurie (2004). "Historians and Their Information Sources" (PDF). College & Research Libraries. September: 400–25, at 416 n.3, citing U.S. Dept. of Labor, Bureau of Labor Statistics (2003),Occupational Outlook Handbook; Lorenz, C. (2001). "History: Theories and Methods". In Smelser, Neil J.; Bates. International Encyclopedia of Social and Behavior Sciences

Historians use other types of sources to understand history as well. Secondary sources are written accounts of history based upon the evidence from primary sources. These are sources which, usually, are accounts, works, or research that analyze, assimilate, evaluate, interpret, and/or synthesize primary sources. Tertiary sources are compilations based upon primary and secondary sources and often tell a more generalized account built on the more specific research found in the first two types of sources.[22]

It should be mentioned again that the Hebrew manuscripts that date to the 3rd, 2nd and 1st centuries B.C.E. are copies of what came down from the originals, which date to as early as middle of the 16th century B.C.E. Moreover, the Dead Sea community believed and wrote that Adam was a real historical person, based on their earliest manuscripts.

Manuscript 4QMMT (also known as the Halakhic Letter or the Sectarian Manifesto, later called Some Precepts of the Law) states, "We have written to you so that you should understand the Book of Moses and the Books of the Prophets and David."

This is one of if not the earliest reference to the custom of subdividing the Scriptures into three parts—'the law of Moses, the Prophets, and the Psalms.' It supports Jesus words, "These are My words which I spoke to you while I was still with you, that all things which are written about Me in the Law of Moses and the Prophets and the Psalms must be fulfilled." (Lu 24:44) The Jewish historian Josephus is in harmony with this text as well (I, 38-40 [8]) around the year 100 C.E., as he confirms the close of the Hebrew Scriptures cannon at the time of Malachi. He wrote, "We do not possess myriads of inconsistent books, conflicting with each other. Our books, those which are justly accredited, are but two and twenty [counted as thirty-nine today], and contain the record of all time. Of these, five are the books of Moses, comprising the laws and the traditional history from the birth of man down to the death of the lawgiver. . . . From the death of Moses until Artaxerxes [i.e., 475-424 B.C.E.], who succeeded Xerxes as king of Persia, the prophets subsequent to Moses wrote the history of the events of their own times in

---

[22] User Education Services. "Primary, Secondary and Tertiary Sources". University of Maryland Libraries. Retrieved 10 Jul 2013.

Amsterdam: Elsevier. p. 6871

"Library Guides: Primary, secondary and tertiary sources"

thirteen books. The remaining four books contain hymns to God and precepts for the conduct of human life."

Review Questions

- What eleven Scriptural points point to Adam and Eve being historical persons?

- Has Science Now Caught Up With the Fact That All of Us Descended from the Same Original Parents?

- How does the Bible View Adam?

- How did Jesus himself view the Genesis?

- What Is Recorded History?

- What does the historical method comprise?

CHAPTER 5 Is the Genesis Creation Account a Myth and Legend?

Image 2 Enuma Elish - the Babylonian epic of creation

Genesis 1:1 Updated American Standard Version (UASV)

¹ In the beginning God created the heavens and the earth.

Over the past 200 years, the scientific community and the Bible scholars of Christianity have engaged in battle. Scientists believe they have proved the Genesis account as being nothing more than a myth or legend, being no different from the Ancient Near Eastern Text of the Enuma Elish ("Epic of Creation"). The latter is a story from the eleventh century BCE, which tells of a cosmic conflict between the gods. The young Marduk kills the wicked Tiamat, the mother goddess of the ocean. Marduk then creates the universe out of Tiamat's remains. Because many people have abandoned the belief in a literal creation account of Genesis, one would surmise the atheistic scientific community has won. Sadly, even some Bible scholars have abandoned the creation account found in Genesis.

It is important we resolve this issue, or we may suffer spiritual shipwreck, falling away from the faith. The entire Bible and its writers view the Genesis account as historically true. Therefore, Genesis is much more than a beginning. It is the foundation upon which all Scripture stands. If it is proven to be nothing more than a myth or legend, it would be next to impossible to take any portion of Scripture as being true and the inspired, i.e., the fully inerrant Word of God. Read Genesis chapter one and then we will compare it with creation stories of ancient societies. Are we to believe that Moses, the author of Genesis, simply borrowed from these other accounts?

The Creation of the World

Genesis 1:1-31 Updated American Standard Version (UASV)

The Creation

¹ In the beginning God created the heavens and the earth.

² Now the earth was without form and empty; and darkness was upon the face of the watery deep: and the Spirit of God was moving over the surface of the waters.

First Creation Day

³ And God said, "Let there be light," and there was light. ⁴ And God saw that the light was good; and God separated the light from the darkness. ⁵And God began calling the light Day, and the darkness he called Night. And there came to be evening and there came to be morning, the first day.

Second Creation Day

⁶ And God went on to say, "Let there be an expanse in the middle of the waters, and let there be a separation between the waters and the waters." ⁷And God proceeded to make the expanse, and make a separation between the waters, which were under the expanse and between the waters, which were above the expanse: and it came to be so. ⁸ And God called the expanse Heaven. And there was evening and there was morning, the second day.

Third Creation Day

⁹ And God said, "Let the waters under the heavens be gathered together into one place, and let the dry land appear." And it was so. ¹⁰ God called the dry land Earth, and the waters that were gathered together he called Seas. And God saw that it was good.

¹¹ And God said, "Let the earth sprout vegetation, plants yielding seed, and fruit trees bearing fruit in which is their seed, each according to its kind, on the earth." And it was so. ¹² The earth brought forth vegetation, plants yielding seed according to their own kinds, and trees bearing fruit in which is their seed, each according to its kind. And God saw that it was good. ¹³ And there was evening and there was morning, the third day.

Fourth Creation Day

14 And God said, "Let there be lights in the expanse of the heavens to separate the day from the night. And let them be for signs and for seasons, and for days and years, **15** and let them be lights in the expanse of the heavens to give light upon the earth." And it was so. **16** And God made[23] the two great lights, the greater light to rule the day and the lesser light to rule the night, and the stars. **17** And God set them in the expanse of the heavens to give light on the earth, **18** to rule over the day and over the night, and to separate the light from the darkness. And God saw that it was good. **19** And there was evening and there was morning, the fourth day.

Fifth Creation Day

20 And God said, "Let the waters swarm with swarms of living creatures, and let birds fly above the earth across the expanse of the heavens." **21** So God created the great sea creatures and every living creature that moves, with which the waters swarm, according to their kinds, and every winged bird according to its kind. And God saw that it was good. **22** And God blessed them, saying, "Be fruitful and multiply and fill the waters in the seas, and let birds multiply on the earth." **23** And there was evening and there was morning, the fifth day.

Sixth Creation Day

24 And God said, "Let the earth bring forth living creatures according to their kinds, livestock and creeping things and beasts of the earth according to their kinds." And it was so. **25** And God made the beasts of the earth according to their kinds and the livestock according to their kinds, and everything that creeps on the ground according to its kind. And God saw that it was good.

26 Then God said, "Let us make man in our image, after our likeness. And let them have dominion over the fish of the sea and over the birds of the heavens and over the livestock and over all the earth and over every creeping thing that creeps on the earth."

27 So God created man in his own image,
in the image of God he created him;
male and female he created them.

---

[23] "And God **made**." Heb., wai**yaas** (from asah). Different from "create" (bara) found in vss 1, 21, 27; 2:3. Progressive action indicated by the imperfect state.

28 And God blessed them. And God said to them, "Be fruitful and multiply and fill the earth and subdue it, and have dominion over the fish of the sea and over the birds of the heavens and over every living thing that moves on the earth." **29** And God said, "Behold, I have given you every plant yielding seed that is on the face of all the earth, and every tree with seed in its fruit. You shall have them for food. **30** And to every beast of the earth and to every bird of the heavens and to everything that creeps on the earth, everything that has the breath of life, I have given every green plant for food." And it was so. **31** And God saw everything that he had made, and behold, it was very good. And there was evening and there was morning, the sixth day.

Ancient Creation Stories[24]

As we discussed in our opening paragraph, the main creation story comes from the Ancient Near Eastern Text of the Enuma Elish, "Epic of Creation."

> One of the best-known of the ancient texts, Enuma Elish gets its title from the first words of the text, often translated "When on high." This text, dated to the end of the second millennium BC, is a hymn commemorating the elevation of Marduk to the head of the pantheon. It includes some of the most detailed information about divine conflict and about cosmology available from ancient Mesopotamia. The first tablet opens with a cosmogony [study of the origin of the universe] / theogony [origin of gods] and introduces Tiamat in conflict with the gods and the slaying of Apsu, interwoven with the account of Marduk's birth. The conflict escalates in tablet two as Tiamat and the rebels threaten the gods. Marduk is finally selected as the champion of the gods with the understanding that if he wins he will be elevated to the head of the pantheon. All the negotiations and preparations come to a climax in tablet four as Marduk defeats Tiamat and lays out the cosmos [universe] using Tiamat's corpse. Establishing the functions of the cosmos

---

[24] A myth is s traditional story about heroes or supernatural beings, often attempting to explain the origins of natural phenomena or aspects of human behavior. "It is generally understood that myths are stories in which the gods are the main characters. Since most people do not believe that "the gods" exist, they consider these stories fanciful and fictional."—John H. Walton. Ancient Near Eastern Thought and the Old Testament: Introducing the Conceptual World of the Hebrew Bible (Kindle Locations 367-368). Kindle Edition.

continues into tablet six and concludes with the creation of people from the blood of Tiamat's partner, Kingu, and the building of Babylon and a temple for Marduk. Tablet seven draws the piece to a conclusion as the fifty names of Marduk are proclaimed to name his attributes, delineate his jurisdiction, and identify his prerogatives.[25]

Genesis 1:3-31 gives the reader an outline of the six creative days and the basic events and creative activities on those days. Genesis 1:1-2 informs the reader of the creation of the heavens and the earth. God proceeded to prepare the earth for human beings. On the first creative day, God said, "'Let there be light,' and there was light." On the second creative day, he formed the expanse above the earth, with water both above and beneath the expanse. The third creative day he formed the dry ground, as well as vegetation and fruit trees. After that, on the fourth day, the sun, moon and stars were now discernible so too served "as signs and for seasons and for days and years." On the fifth day, God caused the waters to "swarm with living creatures, and let birds fly above the earth across the expanse of the sky." Then, God brought forth the land animals and mankind on the sixth creative day.

The question that begs to be answered is: 'Does it seem reasonable the Genesis creation account is based on the above-mentioned creation story?' The comparison of these two accounts ends with some similarities. The creative acts in both accounts are in a similar sequence: firmament, dry land, celestial luminaries, and humans. Both accounts start with a watery chaos and Genesis ends with God at rest and Enuma Elish with the gods at rest. These similarities are not because Moses borrowed from the Ancient Near East, but because they are both based on an actual historical account. The Genesis account is God revealing the true historical events to us, while other creation accounts are an embellishment of those historical events. While we have not read the complete Enuma Elish account, there are numerous differences as well. The almighty God of the Genesis account is nothing like the terrified, quarreling, and vulgar gods of *Enuma Elish*. There is no evidence the Genesis account is dependent on such stories as the Enuma Elish account, but rather the other Ancient Near Eastern stories are based on the Genesis account, which they have simply embellished, leaving only remnants of similarities.

---

[25] John H. Walton. *Ancient Near Eastern Thought and the Old Testament: Introducing the Conceptual World of the Hebrew Bible* (Kindle Locations 410-417). Kindle Edition.

Old Testament Archaeologist Alfred J Hoerth writes,

Archaeologists cannot excavate remains of creation, but from texts like these [Enuma Elish], they know what other ancient cultures had to say about first things. Archaeology does not show that while the biblical account may not be as complete as some might wish,[26] it owes nothing to other ancient cultures or their myths. The complete Enuma Elish reveals much dissimilarity with Genesis. The omnipotent God in Genesis is very unlike the frightened, feuding, and foul gods of the epic. Necessarily there are similarities, but the Genesis account shows no dependence. The fledgling Hebrew nation should have been thankful when God brought them out from the "bewildering variety" of opinions on their origin and, through Moses, told the story as it happened. Viewed only as a creation story, Genesis is not unique, but viewed in comparison with these other stories, Genesis is Lucid and complete. (Hoerth 1998, 187)

---

[26] The Genesis creation account, in fact, the Bible was not written as a science textbook. If God had written exactly how he created the universes, formed the earth to be inhabited, and brought about animal and human life, (1) how many thousands of pages would that have taken, (2) and no one would have understood the science of it for 3,500 years or more, (3) and it would have altered human history.

Review Questions

- Are we to believe that Moses, the author of Genesis, simply borrowed from these other accounts? Explain

- Does it seem reasonable the Genesis creation account is based on the above-mentioned creation story?

CHAPTER 6 Going Back to the Beginning

Image 3 In the beginning God created the heavens and the earth.

Genesis 1:1 Updated American Standard Version (UASV)

¹ In the beginning, God created the heavens and the earth.

What do we learn from this one little phrase? **First**, the universe had a beginning. **Second**, since Jehovah God is the Creator of the Universe, then his existence is outside of creation, In other words, God is existing outside the material universe and so not limited by it. He is beyond, outside of his creation. **Third**, prior to the creation account of the universe, there was no matter and energy. Rather, the universe was created from nothing. **Fourth**, before Genesis 1:1 activity, there was no time as we know it. **Fifth**, God is the sovereign of the universe, and it is him alone that sets the laws and standards that exist under the umbrella of that sovereignty. The 24 elders on the Revelation of John proclaim, "Worthy are you, our Lord and God, to receive glory and honor and power, for you created all things, and by your will they existed and were created." (Rev. 4:11) It is beyond science as to how matter and energy came into existence, because what they do know by natural law (thermodynamics), 'energy cannot be created or destroyed.' All science can do is accept the matter and energy are givens. On the other hand, God's Word is clear that he supernaturally created matter, energy, space, and time as well as the laws that govern them.

Genesis 1:2 Updated American Standard Version (UASV)

2 Now the earth was without form and empty; and darkness was upon the face of the watery deep: and the Spirit of God was moving over the surface of the waters.

In order to deal with the scientific view that the universe is 20 billion years old, they would postulate that that time is to be found between Genesis 1:1 and 1:2. This is why in some translations; you find a space between verse 1 and verse 2, which is known as the Gap Theory (or Restitution Theory).[27] There is no reason to suggest such an idea, it is simply that God by way of his human author, Moses, informed the readers of the creation of the universe, followed by the condition of the earth, before God turn his attention to carrying out acts of creation on the earth, to prepare it for human habitation. According to verses 1 and 2, the universe, which includes the earth was in existence for an unknown period of time before God began the creative days.

First Day: Light (1:3–5)

Genesis 1:3-5 Updated American Standard Version (UASV)

3 And God said, "Let there be light," and there was light. **4** And God saw that the light was good; and God separated the light from the darkness. **5**And God began calling the light Day, and the darkness he called Night. And there came to be evening and there came to be morning, the first day.

There are many different interpretations about how long the Genesis creation days were. We are only going to concern ourselves with two, because one is the orthodox position, the other is the second most

---

[27] This is "as if some great catastrophe (presumably the fall of Satan and his banishment to Earth) befell Earth after its original perfect and complete creation. On this view the six days of creation actually represent the re-creation of the world after its original demise. This view is not widely supported today because it is neither consistent with the grammar of the text nor supportable from the scientific evidence. Nonetheless, it is impossible to know how much (if any) time elapsed between verses 1 and 2." (Whorton 2008)

common position and the position of the author. For a discussion of the length of the Genesis day, please see the first difficulty in the Bible Difficulties in Genesis, Genesis 1:1 Is the earth only 6,000 to 10,000 years old? Are the creative days literally, only 24 hours long? Keep in mind that a different interpretation of this does not alter the inerrancy of Scripture, because it is an interpretation of Scripture, not an error in Scripture. Also, you can listen to the evidence, and make the decision for yourself.

When we look at verses 2-5 of Genesis chapter 1, we need to appreciate that this is not the birth of the sun and the moon; they were there in outer space long before that first creative day. However, they would not have been visible until this time, if one were on the earth. Now, on this first creative day, light evidently punched through the expanse that surrounded the earth, so that it would have been visible to an earthly observer, had there been one. Thus, there was now an evening and there was morning, the first day, because of the rotating earth.

Second Day: The Expanse (1:6–8)

Genesis 1:6-8 Updated American Standard Version (UASV)

⁶ And God went on to say, "Let there be an expanse in the middle of the waters, and let there be a separation between the waters and the waters." ⁷And God proceeded to make the expanse, and make a separation between the waters, which were under the expanse and between the waters, which were above the expanse: and it came to be so. ⁸ And God called the expanse Heaven. And there was evening and there was morning, the second day.

Some older translations like the King James Version and the American Standard Version reads "let there be a firmament." Modern translations read like the ESV, "let there be an expanse." Bible critics tried to use the rendering "firmament" to say that the Bible writers borrowed from the creation myths, as some are picture with this "firmament" as a metal dome. However, even within the King James Version, the marginal reading is "firmament." The Hebrew word, *raqia*, for "expanse" means, "to spread out, stamp, or expand."

We do not understand how the Almighty God bright this separation about, pushing the waters up from the earth, until the circle of the earth was surrounded by "waters that were above the expanse." Genesis 1:20 reads "let birds fly above the earth across the expanse of the heavens."

What took place on the second "day"? How have Bible critics tried to us the poor translation of the Hebrew word for "expanse"? What picture can you draw in your mind as God accomplished the separation of the waters from the waters?

Third Day (a): Land (1:9–10)

Genesis 1:9-10 Updated American Standard Version (UASV)

⁹ And God said, "Let the waters under the heavens be gathered together into one place, and let the dry land appear." And it was so. ¹⁰ God called the dry land Earth, and the waters that were gathered together he called Seas. And God saw that it was good.

Again, we should not expect Moses to disclose explicit detail as to how this was accomplished. However, we can see the exercise of great power on the part of God, as we are being informed about incredible earth movements in the formation of land areas. The geologist, who studies the structure of the earth, would see verses 9-10 as a series of sudden violent catastrophes. Moses, on the other hand, indicates clear direction and control by our Creator, as he formed the earth to be inhabited.

In the book of Job, He questions God. Therefore, God takes Job to task over the creation account, by asking Job numerous questions that emphasize the greatness of God over against man. Where was Job when the earth was created? Can job measure the earth? How is it that the earth just hangs in the sky?

Job 38:3-6 Updated American Standard Version (UASV)

³ Now gird up your loins like a man;
I will question you, and you inform me.

⁴ "Where were you when I laid the foundation of the earth?
Tell me, if you have understanding.
⁵ Who set its measurements? Since you know.
Or who stretched the measuring line upon it?
⁶ On what were its bases sunk?
Or who laid its cornerstone,²⁸

---

²⁸ **38:3 I will question you**. God silenced Job's presumption in constantly wanting to ask questions of God, by becoming Job's questioner. It is important to note that God never told Job about the reason for his pain, i.e., the conflict between Himself and Satan,

Third Day (b): Vegetation (1:11-13)

Genesis 1:11 Updated American Standard Version (UASV)

[11] And God said, "Let the earth sprout vegetation, plants yielding seed, and fruit trees bearing fruit in which is their seed, each according to its kind, on the earth." And it was so.

The light from the sun was now coming through the expanse much stronger by this time, to the point of photosynthesis, which is an absolute need to green plants. This is the process by which green plants and other organisms turn carbon dioxide and water into carbohydrates and oxygen, using light energy trapped by chlorophyll.

Fourth Day: Sun, Moon, and Stars, (1:14–19)

Genesis 1:3, 5 Updated American Standard Version (UASV)

[3] And God said,[29] "**Let there be light**," and there was light. [5] And God began calling the light Day, and the darkness he called Night. And there came to be evening and there came to be morning, **the first day**.

Genesis 1:16, 19 Updated American Standard Version (UASV)

[16] And **God made the two great lights**, the greater light to rule the day and the lesser light to rule the night, and the stars. [19] And there was evening and there was morning, **the fourth day**.

In the above there appears to be a Bible difficulty, in that Genesis 1:3, 5 informs the reader that God brought about light during the first creation day, when he said: "'Let there be light,' and there was light." Then, Genesis 1:16, 19 informs the reader that "God made the two great lights" during the fourth creation day. Hence, did God create or make light on the first or fourth creation day? Before we begin to answer this difficulty, we must bear in mind that Genesis was written from a human

---

which was the reason for Job's suffering. He never did give Job any explanation about the circumstances of his trouble. He simply asked Job if he was as eternal, great, powerful, wise, and perfect as God. If not, Job would have been better off to keep quiet and trust Him. **38:4–38** God asked Job if he participated in creation as He did. That was a crushing, humbling query with an obvious "no" answer. **38:4–7** Creation is spoken of using the language of building construction.–MacArthur, John (2005-05-09). *The MacArthur Bible Commentary* (Kindle Locations 20605-20607). Thomas Nelson. Kindle Edition.

[29] "And God **said**." Heb., wai**yomer**. The first of more than 40 cases in Genesis chapter 1 of progressive action indicated by a Hebrew verb in the imperfect state.

perspective, as an earthly observer, as if he were there; not from a heavenly observation.

In looking at the fourth creation day first, we see that the "greater light" for ruling the day is our sun, and the "lesser light" for ruling the night is our moon. A further explanation of this is found at Psalm 136:7-9 (ASV): "To him that made great lights; for his loving-kindness endures forever: The sun to rule by day; for his loving-kindness endures forever; the moon and stars to rule by night; for his loving-kindness endures forever."

Returning to the first creation day, we find the expression: "let there be light." *Ohr* is the Hebrew word for light, which conveys the idea of light in a broad sense. However, for the fourth creation day, a different word is chosen, *maohr*, which refers to a source of light. Rotherham, in a footnote on "Luminaries" in the *Emphasised Bible*, says: "In ver. 3, 'ôr [ohr], light diffused." Then he goes on to show that the Hebrew word *maohr* in verse 14 has the sense of something "affording light." In other words, on the first creation day *ohr* (light) was spread throughout the earth's atmosphere (being diffused). To an earthly observer, had he been there: he would have not been able to discern the source of light. However, by the fourth creation day, the observer would have been able to see the *maohr* (source) of that light, as the atmosphere would have changed.

It should also be noted that Genesis 1:16 does not use the Hebrew verb *bara*, meaning, "create." Instead, the Hebrew verb *asah* is used, meaning, "make." The reason being, Genesis 1:1 informs us "God created the heavens (which would include sun, moon and stars) and the earth." In other words, the "greater light" (sun) and the "lesser light" (moon) were created long before the fourth creation day. What we have on the fourth creation day is Jehovah God "making" the "greater light" and the "lesser light" to exist in a new way with the surface of the earth and the expanse that had now dissipated even further, allowing the source of light to be seen from earth. God said, "Let there be lights in the expanse of the heavens . . ." (Gen 1:14) This being a further indication of their discernibleness. In addition, they were "to separate the day from the night. And let them be for signs and for seasons, and for days and years." These were to evidence the existence of God and draw attention to his great power, as well as lead man in numerous ways.

Those who steadfastly argue for the young earth view in light of all the evidence against the, here again, this creates a problem, because they also argue that the earth's sun was not created until the fourth day, it literally did not exist until the fourth day. Some suggest that the light from the first creation day was not from our sun but from another source, maybe a temporary light source, or the illumination of God himself. The problem with this, there literal 24 hour days for the first three days had solar days, because they see the text "there was evening and there was morning" as literal. How do you have solar days for three creation days, without our sun? If these three creative days are not defined boy our sun, then the length of those days are unclear. As you can see, this is just another monumental difficulty for those that would take the creation account to be literal, when it was not meant to be taken that way.

Fifth Day: Sea Animals and Birds, (1:20–23)

Genesis 1:20-23 Updated American Standard Version (UASV)

20 And God said, "Let the waters swarm with swarms of living creatures, and let birds fly above the earth across the expanse of the heavens." **21** So God created the great sea creatures and every living creature that moves, with which the waters swarm, according to their kinds, and every winged bird according to its kind. And God saw that it was good. **22** And God blessed them, saying, "Be fruitful and multiply and fill the waters in the seas, and let birds multiply on the earth." **23** And there was evening and there was morning, the fifth day.

The literal translations here decided to be a little more dynamic equivalent in their rendering of the Hebrew nephesh chaiyah, living soul. The term applies to the creatures in the sea, as well as the birds 'flying above the earth across the expanse of the heavens.' This would also apply to the fossil remains of sea monsters that have been discovered in recent times. If we are to fully understand the soul, it would be best to render the Hebrew nephesh (soul) and the Greek Psyche (soul) literally.

Sixth Day: Land Animals and Man, (1:24–31)

Genesis 1:24-31 Updated American Standard Version (UASV)

24 And God said, "Let the earth bring forth living creatures according to their kinds, livestock and creeping things and beasts of the earth according to their kinds." And it was so. **25** And God made the beasts of the earth according to their kinds and the livestock according to their kinds, and everything that creeps on the ground according to its kind. And God saw that it was good.

26 Then God said, "Let us make man in our image, after our likeness. And let them have dominion over the fish of the sea and over the birds of the heavens and over the livestock and over all the earth and over every creeping thing that creeps on the earth."

27 So God created man in his own image,
in the image of God he created him;
male and female he created them.

28 And God blessed them. And God said to them, "Be fruitful and multiply and fill the earth and subdue it, and have dominion over the fish of the sea and over the birds of the heavens and over every living thing that moves on the earth." **29** And God said, "Behold, I have given you every plant yielding seed that is on the face of all the earth, and every tree with seed in its fruit. You shall have them for food. **30** And to every beast of the earth and to every bird of the heavens and to everything that creeps on the earth, everything that has the breath of life, I have given every green plant for food." And it was so. **31** And God saw everything that he had made, and behold, it was very good. And there was evening and there was morning, the sixth day.

As you can see on the sixth creation day we are introduced to the creation of both domestic and wild animals, these being in relation to what man could tame and use domestically, as opposed to what remain wild. Within this creation period was also the greatest of all creation, the creation of both man and woman. It with the creation of humans alone that it was said they were 'created in the image of God.'

Review Questions

- From whose standpoint are the Genesis events described?

- How is the earth described before the first "day"?

- What indication is there in the creation account itself that the word "day" does not mean just a 24-hour period?

- What is one meaning of the Hebrew word for "day" that indicates longer periods can be understood?

- Why does the use of "evening" and "morning" not necessarily limit a "day" to 24 hours?

- What came to be on the first "day," and is Genesis saying that the sun and moon were created at that time?

- What is described for the second "day"? How has the Hebrew word for this development sometimes been mistranslated, and what does it really mean?

- How is the third "day" described?

- What points were raised to Job about the earth?

- What divisions in time became possible by the appearance of the luminaries in the expanse?

- How did the light of the fourth "day" differ from that of the first?

- What kinds of creatures were said to appear on the fifth "day," and within what limits would they reproduce?

- What were the creatures that appeared on the fifth "day" called?

- What took place on the sixth "day"?

CHAPTER 7 Bible Difficulties in Genesis Chapters 1 - 4

Genesis 1:10 Is the Hebrew word for "earth" the same here as is used at Genesis 1:1, and do they mean the same thing?

The Hebrew word is erets in both verse 1 and verse 10. Erets refers to **(1)** earth, as contrasted to the heavens (Gen 1:1); **(2)** or more restricted to all the dry land of the earth (1:10); **(3)** or restricted even further by referring to just the land of a certain section of the earth (Gen 10:10); **(4)** or ground (Gen 1:26); **(5)** or people of the human race (Gen 18:25).

Many people do not realize that all words have more than one sense (meaning). The context will determine which sense belongs to the use under consideration. Even if we were to consider the word "mean," we cannot ascertain what we mean by "mean" outside its context. She says she is resigning, and I think this time she *means* it, would be an expression of intention. I do not know what half these words *mean*, is indicating a particular sense. That is not quite what I *meant*, is intent. Then, let us go to what the dictionary actually considers another word, but spelled the same way. You hurt her feelings, which was a *mean* thing to do. He plays a *mean* sax, which is used in the sense of being skillful. This is the *meanest* climate I have ever lived in, which means uncomfortable. Moreover, we could even look at another term, which is spelled the same, but considered a different word from the first two cases of "mean." We need to find the *mean* between these extremes.

According to A Hebrew and English Lexicon of the Old Testament (Gesenius, Brown, Driver, and Briggs; 1951) erets means: "1. a. earth, whole earth ([as opposed] to a part) . . . b. earth, [as opposed] to heaven, sky . . . c. earth=inhabitants of earth . . . 2. Land = a. country, territory . . . b. district, region . . . 3. a. ground, surface of ground . . . b. soil, as productive." Old Testament Word Studies by William Wilson says of erets, "The earth in the largest sense, both the habitable and uninhabitable parts; with some accompanying word of limitation, it is used of some portion of the earth's surface, a land or country." Therefore, the first and primary meaning of the Hebrew word is our planet, or globe, the earth.

(erets) in verses 10-12 is "land," while in verses 1-2 it was "earth." Recognizing this relieves us of the problems in Paul Seely, "The Geographical Meaning of `Earth' and `Seas' in Genesis 1:10," Westminster Theological Journal 59 (1997): 231-55, who takes [erets] as the entire earth, a flat disk of ancient conception.[30]

Genesis 1:16 Was light created or made, and was it on the first day or the fourth?

Genesis 1:3, 5 American Standard Version (ASV)

[3]And God said, **Let there be light**: and there was light. [5]And God called the light Day, and the darkness he called Night. And there was evening and there was morning, **one day**.

Genesis 1:3, 5 New American Standard Bible (NASB)

[3]Then God said, "**Let there be light**"; and there was light. [5]God called the light day, and the darkness He called night And there was evening and there was morning, **one day**.

Genesis 1:3, 5 English Standard Version (ESV)

[3]And God said, "**Let there be light**," and there was light. [5]And there was evening and there was morning, **the first day**.

Genesis 1:3, 5 New International Version (NIV)

[3]And God said, "**Let there be light**," and there was light. [5]God called the light "day," and the darkness he called "night." And there was evening, and there was morning—**the first day**.

Genesis 1:3, 5 Holman Christian Standard Bible (HCSB)

[3]Then God said, "**Let there be light**," and there was light. [5]God called the light "day," and He called the darkness "night." Evening came, and then morning: **the first day**.

Genesis 1:16, 19 American Standard Version (ASV)

[16]And **God made the two great lights**; the greater light to rule the day, and the lesser light to rule the night: he made the stars also. [19]And there was evening and there was morning, **a fourth day**.

---

[30] C. John Collins. Genesis 1-4: A Linguistic, Literary, And Theological Commentary (Kindle Locations 3685-3687). Kindle Edition.

Genesis 1:16, 19 New American Standard Bible (NASB)

[16]**God made the two great lights**, the greater light to govern the day, and the lesser light to govern the night; He made the stars also. [19]There was evening and there was morning, **a fourth day**.

Genesis 1:16, 19 English Standard Version (ESV)

[16]And **God made the two great lights**—the greater light to rule the day and the lesser light to rule the night—and the stars. [19]And there was evening and there was morning, **the fourth day**.

Genesis 1:16, 19 New International Version (NIV)

[16]**God made two great lights**—the greater light to govern the day and the lesser light to govern the night. He also made the stars. [19]And there was evening, and there was morning—**the fourth day**.

Genesis 1:16, 19 Holman Christian Standard Bible (HCSB)

[16] **God made the two great lights**—the greater light to have dominion over the day and the lesser light to have dominion over the night—as well as the stars. [19]Evening came, and then morning: **the fourth day**.

In the above there appears to be a difficulty, in that Genesis 1:3, 5 informs the reader that God brought about light during the first creation day, when he said: "'Let there be light,' and there was light." Then, Genesis 1:16, 19 informs the reader that "God made the two great lights" during the fourth creation day. Hence, did God create or make light on the first or fourth creation day? Before we begin to answer this difficulty, we must bear in mind that Genesis was written from a human perspective, as an earthly observer, as if he were there; not from a heavenly observation.

In looking at the fourth creation day first, we see that the "greater light" for ruling the day is our sun, and the "lesser light" for ruling the night is our moon. A further explanation of this is found at Psalm 136:7-9 (ASV): "To him that made great lights; for his loving-kindness endures forever: The sun to rule by day; for his loving-kindness endures forever; the moon and stars to rule by night; for his loving-kindness endures forever."

Returning to the first creation day, we find the expression: "let there be light." *Ohr* is the Hebrew word for light, which conveys the idea of light in a broad sense. However, for the fourth creation day, a different word is chosen, *maohr*, which refers to a source of light. Rotherham, in a footnote on "Luminaries" in the *Emphasised Bible*, says: "In ver. 3, '*ôr* ['*ohr*], light diffused." Then he goes on to show that the Hebrew word *maohr* in verse 14 has the sense of something "affording light." In other words, on the first creation day *ohr* (light) was spread throughout the earth's atmosphere (being diffused). To an earthly observer, had he been there: he would have not been able to discern the source of light. However, by the fourth creation day, the observer would have been able to see the *maohr* (source) of that light, as the atmosphere would have changed.

It should also be noted that Genesis 1:16 does not use the Hebrew verb bara, meaning, "create." Instead, the Hebrew verb asah is used, meaning, "make." The reason being, Genesis 1:1 informs us "God created the heavens (which would include sun, moon and stars) and the earth." In other words, the "greater light" (sun) and the "lesser light" (moon) were created long before the fourth creation day. What we have on the fourth creation day is Jehovah God "making" the "greater light" and the "lesser light" to exist in a new way with the surface of the earth and the expanse that had now dissipated even further, allowing the source of light to be seen from earth. God said, "Let there be lights in the expanse of the heavens . . ." (Gen 1:14) This being a further indication of their discernibleness. In addition, they were "to separate the day from the night. And let them be for signs and for seasons, and for days and years." These were to evidence the existence of God and draw attention to His great power, as well as lead man in numerous ways.

Genesis 1-2 Is there a Different order of creation in Genesis 2 than Genesis 1?

Genesis 1:1-2 inform the reader of the creation of the heavens and the earth. **Genesis 1:3-31** gives the reader an outline of the six creative days and the basic events and creative activities on those days. **Genesis 2:1-3** is some basics on the seventh day, while **Genesis 2:4** is a summary verse of the whole six creative days. Genesis **chapter 2:5-25** is a parallel account that picks up the account, not on the first day, but the third day (after the land comes on the scene, but prior to the creation of land plants), adding details. **(2:5-6)** This chapter is used to give more details about the human creation. For example, there is no simple statement that Adam was created; it adds that he was formed out of the dust of the ground, with the breath of life being blown into him, his becoming a living soul. **(2:7)** It informs of the planting of the Garden of Eden and placing Adam in it. **(2:8)** We learn of the growth of many trees for food, tree of life, and the tree of knowledge of good and bad. **(2:9)** We are even given geographical sites that help the readers of Moses day, to know where the Garden of Eden was. **(2:10-14)** We are told of the work assignments given to Adam, to cultivate the Garden of Eden and to name the animals. **(2:15, 19-20)** We are informed of the prohibition of eating from the tree of knowledge of good and bad. **(2:16-17)** Then, we are informed that Adam grew lonely from his naming the animals, as he saw all of them had mates. **(2:18, 20)** From there the reader gets a detailed account of the creation of Eve **(2:21-22)**, and Adam's response, with the Jehovah, in essence, performing the first marriage. **(2:23-25)** Therefore, as you can see, **chapter 1** is the barest of outlines, with **chapter 2** giving us details about the arrival of the humans. **Chapter 3:1-24** deals with the temptation of Eve by the serpent and the sinning of both Adam and Eve, with the terrible consequences of that willful rebellion.

Genesis 1:26 Who are the "us" and "our" of this verse

Genesis 1:26-27 English Standard Version (ESV)

[26]Then God said, "Let us make man in our image, after our likeness. And let them have dominion over the fish of the sea and over the birds of the heavens and over the livestock and over all the earth and over every creeping thing that creeps on the earth."

[27]So God created man in his own image,

in the image of God he created him;

male and female he created them.

Different Bible scholars have offered up different interpretations over the last 2,000 years, one of which is that God is here referring to himself and the angels. However, this does not seem like a good option based on the context. If you will look at verse 26 again, you will see that God says, "Let us make man in our image" while verse 27 clearly states, "God created man in his own image," not the image of angels.

While it is true that the plural pronoun "us" is required because of the plural noun elohim (God): "Then God [elohim, plural] said, "Let us [plural] make man in our image." There are a couple points to keep in mind: **(1)** the plural ending "im" on elohim is majestic, expressing the majesty of God, not expressing multiple persons; **(2)** however, it is quite clear from Scripture that God's only-begotten Son was involved in the creation of man with his heavenly Father, as the Father's master worker. (John 1:3; 1:18; Col 1:15-16; Pro 8:21-22, 30-31, NASB) Therefore, the plural "us" and "our" simply means that two or more persons were involved. Therefore, when God used "us" and "our," he was merely addressing another person, the prehuman Jesus prior to his ascension to earth, the master workman of Proverbs 8:22-31, "the firstborn of all creation. For by him all things were created, in heaven and on earth, visible and invisible." Colossians 1:15-16.

Genesis 2:4 "God" is used in Genesis chapter 1, while chapter 2 changes to Jehovah God. Does this mean that there are two different authors?

The higher critics argue that every Bible verse that contains the Hebrew word for God, (*Elohim*), set off by itself has its own writer, designated by the capital "E" ("Elohist"). On the other hand, any verse that contains the Tetragrammaton, (Jehovah, Yahweh), God's personal name, is attributed to yet another writer, "J" ("Jawist"). (Cassuto, 18-21) Let us see how they explain this. The critics argue that "God" (*Elohim*) is restricted in use exclusively in the first chapter of Genesis (1:1–31) in relation to God's creation activity, and that starting in Genesis 2:4 through the end of the second chapter we find God's personal name.

R. E. Friedman speaks of a discovery by three men: "One was a minister, one was a physician, and one was a professor. The discovery that they made ultimately came down to the combination of two pieces of evidence: doublets and the names of God. They saw that there were apparently two versions each of a large number of Biblical stories: two accounts of the creation, two accounts each of several stories about the patriarchs Abraham and Jacob, and so on. Then, they noticed that, quite often, one of the two versions of a story would refer to God by one name and the other version would refer to God by a different name." (R. E. Friedman, 50)

Different settings, however, require different uses. This principle holds true throughout the whole of the entire Old Testament. Moses may choose to use (*Elohim*) in a setting in which he wants to show a particular quality clearly, like power, creative activity, and so on. On the other hand, Moses may choose to use God's personal name (Jehovah, Yahweh) when the setting begs for that personal relationship between the Father and his children, the Israelites, or even more personable, a one-on-one conversation between Jehovah God and a faithful servant.

The Divine Names: The weakness of claiming multiple authors because of the different names used for God is quite evident when we look at just one small portion of the book of Genesis in the *American Standard Version* (1901). God is called "God Most High," "possessor (or maker) of heaven and earth," "O Lord Jehovah," "a God that seeth," "God Almighty," "God," "[the] God,"[31] and "the Judge of all the earth." (Genesis 14:18, 19; 15:2; 16:13; 17:1, 3; 18:25) It is difficult to believe that different authors wrote these verses. Moreover, let us take a look at Genesis 28:13, which says: "And, behold, Jehovah stood above it, and said, I am Jehovah, the God ["Elohim"] of Abraham thy father, and the God of Isaac: the land whereon thou liest, to thee will I give it, and to thy seed." Another scripture, Psalm 47:5, says: "God is gone up with a shout, Jehovah with the sound of a trumpet."[32] (*ASV*) In applying their documentary analysis, we would have to accept the idea that two authors worked together on each of these two verses.

Many conservative scholars have come to realize that in a narrative format one will often find a ruler being referred to not only by name, but also by a title, such as "king." M. H. Segal observes: "Just as those interchanges of human proper names and their respective appellative common nouns cannot by any stretch of the imagination be ascribed to a change of author or source of document, so also the corresponding interchanges of the divine names in the Pentateuch must not be attributed to such a literary cause."* If one were to look up "Adolf Hitler" using *Academic American Encyclopedia*, within three paragraphs he will find the terms "Führer," "Adolf Hitler," and simply "Hitler." Who is so bold as to suggest that there are three different authors for these three paragraphs?

Dr. John J. Davis[33] helps us to appreciate that there is "no other religious document from the ancient Near East [that] was compiled in such a manner; a documentary analysis of the Gilgames Epic or Enuma Elis would be complete folly. The author of Genesis may have selected divine names on the basis of theological emphasis rather than dogmatic preference. Many divine names were probably interchangeable; Baal and

---

[31] The title Elohim preceded by the definite article ha, giving the expression ha Elohim.

32. See also Psalm 46:11; 48:1, 8.

33. John J. Davis, *Paradise to Prison: Studies in Genesis* (Salem: Sheffield, 1975), 22–23.

Hadad were used interchangeably in the Hadad Tablet from Ugarit[34] and similar examples could be cited from Egyptian texts."[35]

In fact, we now know that there were many deities in the ancient Near East that had multiple names. As stated above with the Babylonian Creation account, the Enuma Elish, the god Marduk (Merodach), chief deity of Babylon, also had some 50 different names.[36] It would not even be thinkable to apply any of the Documentary Hypothesis analysis to any of these works. Why? Not only because we can see that ancient writers are no different than modern writers and are able to use different names and titles interchangeably within their work, but they were written on stone, so to speak. If one has one clay tablet that has both a personal name, and two different titles for the same king, it would be difficult to argue that there were two or three different authors for the one tablet. Bible scholar Mark F. Rooker has the following to say about the use of Elohim and Yahweh in the Old Testament:

Moreover, it is clear that throughout the Old Testament that the occurrence of the names of God as Elohim or Yahweh is to be attributed to contextual and semantic issues, not the existence of sources. This conclusion is borne out by the fact that the names consistently occur in predictable genre. In the legal and prophetic texts the name Yahweh always appears, while in wisdom literature the name for God is invariably Elohim. In narrative literature, which includes much of the Pentateuch, both Yahweh and Elohim are used.[37*] Yet consistently the names do not indicate different sources but were chosen by design. The name Elohim was used in passages to express the abstract idea of Deity as evident in God's role as Creator of the universe and the Ruler of nature. Yahweh, on the other hand, is the special covenant name of God who has entered into a relationship with the Israelites since the name reflects God's ethical character. (Cassuto, 31) Given the understanding of the meaning of these names for God, it is no wonder that the source which contains the name

---

34 . G. R. Driver, *Canaanite Myths and Legends* (New York: T. & T. Clark, 1971), 70-72.

35. For example, see the "Stele of Ikhernofret" in James B. Pritchard, ed., *Ancient Near Eastern Texts*, 2nd ed. Princeton: Princeton University Press, 1955, pp. 329–30.

36. K. A. Kitchen, *On the Reliability of the Old Testament* (Grand Rapids: Eerdmans, 2003), 424–5.

37 Similarly, Livingston has pointed out that the cognate West Semitic divine names il and ya(w) appear to be interchangeable in the Eblaite tablets. (The Pentateuch in Its Cultural Environment, 224.)

Yahweh would appear to reflect a different theology from a selected group of texts which contained the name Elohim."[38]

Let us, on a small scale, do our own analysis of the divine names in the first two chapters of Genesis. The Hebrew word (*elohim*) is most often agreed upon to be from a root meaning "be strong," "mighty," or "power."[39] It should be said too that by far, most Hebrew scholars recognize the plural form (*im*) of this title *elohim* to be used as a plural of "majesty," "greatness," or "excellence." The Hebrew word (*elohim*) is used for the Creator 35 times from Genesis 1:1 to 2:4a. Exactly what is the context of this use? It is used in a setting that deals with God's power, his greatness, his excellence, his creation activity, all of which seems appropriate, does it not?

Moving on to Genesis 2:4b–25, we find God now being referred to by his personal name, the Tetragrammaton (YHWH, JHVH), which is translated "Jehovah" (*KJV, ASV, NW, NEB*, etc.) or "Yahweh" (*AT, NAB, JB, HCSB*, etc.). It is found in verses 4b–25 a total of 11 times; however, it comes before his title (*elohim*).[40] Why the switch, and what is the context of this use? This personal name of God is used in a setting that deals with his personal relationship with man and woman. This is not a second creation account; it is a more detailed account of the creation of man, which was only briefly mentioned in chapter one in passing, as each feature of creation was ticked off. In chapter two, the Creator becomes a person as he speaks to his intelligent creation, giving them the prospect of an eternal perfect life in a paradise garden, which is to be cultivated earth wide, to be filled with perfect offspring. Therefore, we see a personal interchange between God and man as He lays out His plans to Adam, which seems very appropriate, does it not, when switching from using a title in chapter one to using a personal name in chapter two? In chapter two, we have the coupling of the personal name "Jehovah" with the title "God," to show that we are still talking about this 'great,' 'majestic,' 'all powerful' Creator, but personalized as he introduces himself to his new earthly creation.

Thus, there is no reason to assume that we are talking about two different writers. No, it is two different settings in which a skilled writer

---

38. Mark F. Rooker, *Leviticus: The New American Commentary* (Nashville: Broadman & Holman, 2001), 26–27.

39. Ibid., 27.

40. "Jehovah God." Heb., Yehwah Elohim.

would make the transition just as Moses did. It would be no different from if a modern-day news commentator were giving as a report about the United States President visiting Russia to meet with Dmitry Anatolyevich Medvedev, in which he used the title President predominately. The following week the same news commentator may be covering the President visiting a hospital with injured children who had survived a tornado, and refer to the President as President Obama. It isn't difficult to see that one is an official setting where the President needs to be portrayed as powerful, while in the other setting; he needs to be portrayed as personable. The same principles used herein apply to the rest of the Pentateuch and the Old Testament as a whole.

Genesis 2:8 Was the Garden of Eden a real historical place?

The search for the Garden of Eden has gone on since Noah stepped of the ark. The exact location is speculative at best. Nevertheless, we can infer some things, without going beyond Scripture.

Genesis 2:10-14 Updated American Standard Version (UASV)

10 Now a river flowed out[41] of Eden to water the garden; and from there it divided and became <u>four rivers</u>.[42] **11** The name of the first is <u>Pishon</u>; it flows around the whole land of Havilah, where there is gold. **12** And the gold of that land is good; bdellium and onyx stone are there. **13** The name of the second river is <u>Gihon</u>; it flows around the whole land of Cush. **14** The name of the third river is <u>Tigris</u>; it flows east of Assyria.[43] And the fourth river is the <u>Euphrates</u>.

The Euphrates has long been known, as is also true of the Tigris. However, the identity of the Pishon and Gihon has never been identified. In addition, the topography today does not have the Euphrates and Tigris Rivers proceeding from a single source. The earth wide flood that Noah and his family survived in the ark would explain the change in topography. Some rivers would have been filled in and others would have had their courses changed. Even a tremendous local flood can change the course of a river, such as the Mississippi in the United States.

---

[41] Lit., *was going out*; Hebrew participle refers to a continuous stream

[42] Lit *became four heads*

[43] *Assyria* Heb., *Ashshur*

The long accepted location of the Garden of Eden has been the mountainous area about 140 miles Southwest on Mount Ararat, in the Eastern part of Modern-day Turkey. Again, the mountains could be a result of the flood, or it could be that a mountainous range surrounded the Garden of Eden, giving us the reason why only the East of Eden was protected by cherubs. Genesis 3:24.

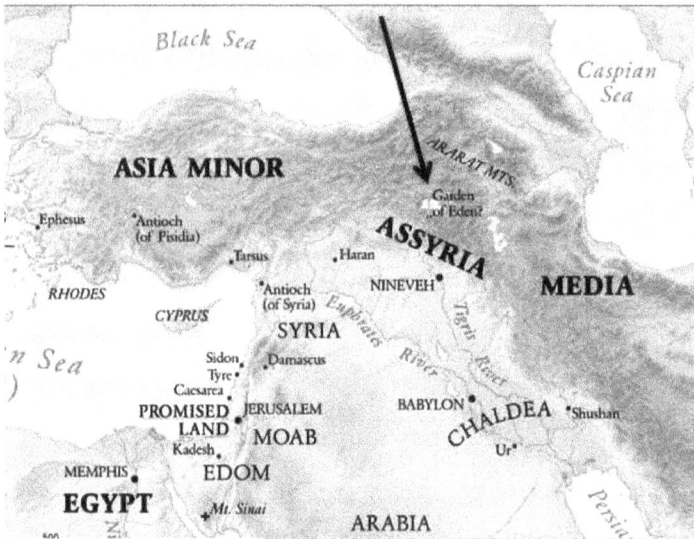

Image 4 it-1 p. 676 Eden

Genesis 2:10-14 Was the mention of Assyria an inaccurate statement?

The account at Genesis 2:10-14 gives geographical details about the Garden of Eden. Moses wrote that one river was "the one going to the east of Assyria." However, the land of Assyria received its name from Asshur, the son of Shem born after the Flood. (Genesis 10:8-11, 22; Ezekiel 27:23; Micah 5:6) Clearly, in his accurate, inspired description, Moses merely used the term "Assyria" to denote to a region that his readers would have been aware of.

Sadly, it is true that most modern scholars dismiss the Garden of Eden as a legend or a myth, not being a real historical account. Nevertheless, this writer, as well as many other conservative scholars, accept the historical reality of the whole of Genesis. The account itself is highly detail, giving the sense of a historical narrative, not a myth or legend. Morever, we do have geographical evidence, as two of the four rivers identified, are still in existence today. In addition verse 14 says, "The name of the third river is the Tigris, which flows east of Assyria. And the fourth river is the Euphrates." This location is present day Iraq.

Genesis 2:17 Why did Adam and Eve not die in the day that they ate of the fruit from the forbidden tree?

God at Genesis 2:17 warned Adam of "the tree of the knowledge of good and evil you shall not eat, for in the day that you eat of it you shall surely die." It would seem that when Adam passed that warning on to Eve, she took it very seriously, because she expanded on and emphasized the warning when speaking with the serpent. The woman said to the serpent, God said, 'You shall not eat of the fruit of the tree that is in the midst of the garden, neither shall you touch it, lest you die.'" (Gen 3:3) You will notice that she added, "neither shall you touch it." "But the serpent said to the woman, "'You will not surely die.'" (Gen 3:4) Was the serpent (i.e., Satan), telling the truth, as Adam would go on to live for another 930-years? (Gen 5:5) No, Satan lied! In the day of their eating the fruit of the forbidden tree, they died spiritually.

If we look at the context of Adam when he received the command at Genesis 2:17, how would have Adam understood the expression, "in the day that you eat of it"? It is true, that Moses said to God, "For a thousand years in your sight are but as yesterday." (Ps 90:4) In addition, while addressing the extent of Jehovah God's patience, the apostle Peter said, "that with the Lord one day is as a thousand years, and a thousand years as one day." (2 Pet 3:8) However, Adam lived and died long before both of these statements, and would have had no knowledge of such. It was not as though Adam was thinking of his great love for Eve, and saying to himself, "If I eat of the forbidden tree, I will have one of Jehovah's days to live, a thousand years to spend with Eve. Yes, Adam would have no knowledge with which to reason in such a way. In other words, he would have understood the word "day" to be a literal twenty-four-hour day. God does not speak ambiguously, and he would have expressed himself in order to be understood, according to what Adam would know as to the terms that were used. Thus, God meant exactly what Adam would have understood it to mean, a twenty-four-hour day. God did not mean, "the tree of the knowledge of good and evil you shall not eat, for in the [thousand-year-long day] that you eat of it you shall surely die." Such a statement as that would have had no force in the mind of Adam; it would have lost all intended force of Jehovah's warning.

Adam would have received the Genesis 2:17 warning directly from God, even if a representative, his only-begotten Son, "the Word", delivered that warning.[44] This of course, begs the question, why then did Adam and Eve not die 'in a twenty-four-hour day?' Well, we must ask another question first. As to the Bible, what is death? The World Book Encyclopedia (1987, Vol. 5, p. 52b) pointed out: "A person whose heart and lungs stop working may be considered clinically dead, but somatic death may not yet have occurred. The individual cells of the body continue to live for several minutes. The person may be revived if the heart and lungs start working again and give the cells the oxygen they need. After about three minutes, the brain cells, which are most sensitive to a lack of oxygen, begin to die. The person is soon dead beyond any possibility of revival. Gradually, other cells of the body also die. The last ones to perish are the bone, hair, and skin cells, which may continue to grow for several hours." We know that the breathing and the active life force (Heb., ruach chaiyim) maintained in the cells by the blood is very important. From this, we can see that it is not the termination of breathing and the heartbeat alone, but also includes the loss of the life force from the body's cells that brings the sort of physical death as spoken of in the Scriptures. Ps 104:29; 146:4; Eccl 8:8.

However, the Scriptures speak of another kind of death, a spiritual death, which is illustrated by the death spoken of above as the condition of humankind at present, but is also relative to our discussion as well. In other words, Adam died spiritually in the very day of eating from the forbidden tree, and this would result in old age and eventually death. A man was begging of from following Jesus, saying, "Lord, let me first go and bury my father." Jesus responded, "Leave the dead to bury their own dead. . ." (Lu 9:59-60) The man's father was not dead yet, the son simply wanted to hold off following Jesus until his father died, and was simply looking for a way out. However, Jesus' response, "Leave the dead to bury their own dead," illustrated that spiritually dead and being dead are, in essence, one and the same unless there is some sort of intervention (more on that later), because physical death is the eventuality of those that are spiritually dead.

In addition, we have the apostle Paul referring to the woman living for sensual indulgence as "dead even while she lives." (Lu 9:60; 1Ti 5:6; Eph 2:1) Physical death was the sentence handed down to Adam and thus his descendants as well. However, this was brought about by way of the

---

[44] See question on Genesis 3:8 as to who had spoken directly with Adam.

spiritual death, which affected Adam and Eve the very moment they ate from the forbidden tree. They were now alienated from God, and removed from the symbolic tree of life, being sent out from the Garden of Eden. This alienation is self-evident as the two vainly tried to hide from God, their guilt ridden conscious affecting them. (Gen 3:8) The apostle Paul expressed it as being "dead in the trespasses and sins," becoming "children of wrath." (Eph 2:1–3)

Romans 6:7 says, "one who has died has been set free from sin." However, Roman 6:2, 11 informs us that a Christian can 'consider themselves dead to sin and alive to God in Christ Jesus." Romans 7:2-6 helps us to appreciate that Christians "are released from the law, having died to that which held us captive, so that we serve in the new way of the Spirit and not in the old way of the written code. Jesus said that he came to earth "to give his life as a ransom for many." (Matthew 20:28).

Adam and Eve were guilty before God, and then stood before him in an unrighteous condition. Within this unrighteous condition came a defilement and pollution of a new state of being, fallen flesh (Gr., sarx), which placed Adam and his descendants in an alienated position toward God and in enmity toward him (Rom 8:5-8) Hence, the mindset of imperfect man is mentally bent and geared toward evil. Because of Adam, we are born into sin (missing the mark of perfection), and are looking at the sentence of death. (Ps 51:5; Rom 5:12; Eph 2:3). This was the condition of Adam and Eve, the very moment they willfully chose to rebel against God, and commit that awful transgression. Instantly, they were thrown into the condition of a spiritual death. At that moment there was no hope for the human race, regardless of what any would do in life, the sentence would be death. However, Jehovah is a God of mercy, and while the human race merited death, we received undeserved kindness, which can be found at Genesis 3:15.

As has been stated and is obvious from Scripture, the physical death did not come immediately. God had created them perfectly after all; therefore, they would take far longer to grow older and die. Regardless, they were no longer going to be perfect, but had taken on imperfection. God had removed his blessing of them as being good, and, eventually, their imperfection would show signs of growing old and impending death

The penalty was unavoidable. As to justice, from the viewpoint of God, Adam and Eve died that day. (Compare Luke 20:37-38.) However, to fulfill his own will and purpose regarding the inhabiting of the earth, Jehovah permitted them to produce a family before they were to grow old, get sick and die. All the same, while Adam and Eve may have not been aware of God's viewpoint of time, they both did die within one of his days, a thousand years. While there may be no absolute connection between Moses or Peter's statement about the way God views time, it seems a bit too much, to be a mere coincidence that Adam lived to be 930-years, and Methuselah lived to be 969-years, with not one preflood person living beyond a thousand years old. (Gen. 5:3-5; Ps 90:4; 2 Pet 3:8.).

Genesis 2:17; 3:3 What was the fruit of the tree of the knowledge of good and evil?

Genesis 2:17 Updated American Standard Version (UASV)

[17] but from the tree of the knowledge of good and evil you shall not eat,[45] for in the day that you eat from it you shall surely die."[46]

There were plenty of trees to eat from in the Garden of Eden, more than enough to satisfy the desires of the first human couple. However, there was tree that they were forbidden to eat from, "the tree of the knowledge of good and evil." (Gen 2:17) This probation to not eat from that tree was so serious that Adam must have been very emphatic when he told Eve. How do we know that? We can infer it from Eve's Response to the Serpent when he was tempting her. Eve not only said 'you cannot eat from it,' but also added, "neither shall you touch it, lest you die." (Gen 3:3)

Some have suggested that the prohibition against the fruit of this tree is symbolic, the fruit standing for sexual intercourse. Others have suggested that it stood for having a knowledge of or an awareness of right and wrong. Still others have suggested that it stood for the knowledge that they would have attained upon reaching maturity, by way of experience, which could be used for good or bad. The sexual intercourse can immediately be dismissed, as they were commanded to, "be fruitful, multiply, and fill the earth". (Gen 1:28) The awareness of good and bad must be dismissed as well, because both had that capacity already, as it was good to not eat from the tree, and bad to eat from the tree. Lastly, the idea of it being a sin to acquire knowledge upon reaching maturity, as this would contradict the whole of the rest of God's Word,

---

[45] Lit *eat from it*

[46] Lit *dying you* [singular] *shall die.* Heb *moth tamuth*; the first reference to death in the Scriptures

not to mention the idea of expecting the human creation, He designed to grow and mature, to remain in an immature state, is illogical.

The Bible is silent as to the type of tree. However, the idea of the tree being symbolic is correct. The fruit had no intrinsic power to give knowledge, as was evidenced after their eating from it. It did symbolize God's right of sovereignty, His right to set a standard of what is good and bad. To eat from the tree would have been a rejection of that sovereignty, a rebellion that said that could set their own standard of good and bad, independence from their creator. This was a simple test, for a couple that was to serve as the father and mother of a perfect human race. A footnote on Genesis 2:17, in The Jerusalem Bible (1966):

"This knowledge is a privilege which God reserves to himself and which man, by sinning, is to lay hands on, 3:5, 22. Hence it does not mean omniscience, which fallen man does not possess; nor is it moral discrimination, for unfallen man already had it and God could not refuse it to a rational being. It is the power of deciding for himself what is good and what is evil and of acting accordingly, a claim to complete moral independence by which man refuses to recognize his status as a created being. The first sin was an attack on God's sovereignty, a sin of pride."

Genesis 2:17; 3:3 what did the tree of the knowledge of good and evil symbolize?

There is more involved in Adam and Eve's choice to eat from the "tree of knowledge of good and evil," as being a sin.[47] It is not like the act of a child stealing a piece of fruit off a fruit stand. This was a rebellion against their Creator, Jehovah God. What escapes most humans is that they were created, and there is a Creator. The desire for absolute independence runs contrary to this, and is hard for him to accept. Jehovah God had every right in setting a tree that would establish the point of his sovereignty (right to rule). Adam and Eve were created, and did not have absolute independence and freedom, it was relative to their environment, as created persons, which is a lesson that they needed to understand through more than mere words.

---

[47] 3:3 nor shall you touch it. This appears to be an addition to the original prohibition as recorded (cf. Gen. 2:17). Adam may have so instructed her for her protection. It could also mean that Eve, apparently beginning to feel God's restriction was too harsh, added to the harshness of it.–MacArthur, John (2005-05-09). *The MacArthur Bible Commentary* (Kindle Locations 2063-2065). Thomas Nelson. Kindle Edition.

If perfect humankind were to do as Jehovah had requested, multiply and fill the earth, it would have resulted in a paradise wide planet, filled with perfect human creation. If there was to be universal peace, man needed to appreciate that he had been Created and that he was designed to walk with God, not walk on his own. This would have been established if the first two, especially Adam, were to refrain from eating from the "tree of knowledge of good and evil." Adam was to become the father to all of perfect humankind, and he needed to be loyal to his Creator, proving his obedience, by this one small act of refraining from eating from the forbidden tree.

Luke 16:10 Updated American Standard Version (UASV)

[10] "The one who is faithful in the least thing is also faithful in much, and the one who is unrighteous in what is least is also unrighteous in much.

Both Adam and Eve were able to choose not to eat from the tree. In fact, they were designed in such a way that to do bad would be going against their natural inclinations. Of course, they knew the difference between good and bad. It was bad to eat from the forbidden tree, and it was good to not eat from it. Therefore, it was not a matter of their being ignorant of good and bad, as though God were trying to keep such knowledge from them. Thus, the tree or its fruit had no intrinsic substance, which would wake them up to the idea of what is good and what is bad. The good and bad was the ability to choose what is good and bad. The right and wrong of life belonged under the umbrella of the sovereignty of their Creator, not man. If man lived under the standard of right and wrong of his Creator, all would remain perfect.

A footnote on Genesis 2:17, in The Jerusalem Bible represents well what the tree stood for (1966):

> This knowledge is a privilege which God reserves to himself and which man, by sinning, is to lay hands on, 3:5, 22. Hence it does not mean omniscience, which fallen man does not possess; nor is it moral discrimination, for unfallen man already had it and God could not refuse it to a rational being. It is the power of deciding for himself what is good and what is evil and of acting accordingly, a claim to complete moral independence by which man refuses to recognize his status as a created being. The first sin was an attack on God's sovereignty, a sin of pride.

Genesis 3:5 Is man made in the image of God or does he become like God?

·   We are told at Genesis 1:27 that "God created man in his own image." However, Genesis 3:22 tells us "the man has become like one of us." It seems that Genesis 1:27 is saying that humans *were made* like God, while Genesis 3:22 is saying that humans *became* like God.

The answer lies in the fact that we are dealing with two different subject matters, and to look at the two together isolated from their individual sections is to take them out of context. Genesis 1 is dealing with the creation of humanity, and that we were *made in* the image of God, something we were given. Genesis 3 is dealing with man's fall into sin, and his willful rebellion against God, rejecting God's sovereignty, God's standard of right and wrong. In this, Adam and Eve had acquired the right to *become* like God in determining for themselves what is right and what is wrong. Genesis 1 is prior to the fall, refers to the nature of Adam and Eve, while Genesis 3 is after the fall, and refers to their state of being.

Genesis 3:6 She also gave some to her husband who was with her?

Almost all translations translate Genesis 3:6 as follows.

Genesis 3:6 (ESV)	Genesis 3:6 (LEB)	Genesis 3:6 (ASV)	Genesis 3:6 (NASB)
⁶ So when the woman saw that the tree was good for food, and that it was a delight to the eyes, and that the tree was to be desired to make one wise, **she took of its fruit and ate, and she also gave some to her husband who was with her**, and he ate.	⁶ When the woman saw that the tree was good for food and that it was a delight to the eyes, and the tree was desirable to make one wise, then **she took from its fruit and she ate. And she gave it also to her husband with her**, and he ate.	⁶ And when the woman saw that the tree was good for food, and that it was a delight to the eyes, and that the tree was to be desired to make one wise, **she took of the fruit thereof, and did eat; and she gave also unto her husband with her**, and he did eat.	⁶ When the woman saw that the tree was good for food, and that it was a delight to the eyes, and that the tree was desirable to make one wise, **she took from its fruit and ate; and she gave also to her husband with her**, and he ate.

As you can see from these English translations, the plain sense of the text is, Adam was with her. This creates a real Bible difficulty. Before I delve into why, I will say that if almost all of the translations are in agreement, generally, this should be respected, and accepted. It is very unlikely that the very best Hebrew and Greek scholars of the past 100 years are all mistaken. Now, the difficulty arises because, if Eve and Adam were standing there before the tree of knowledge, as the serpent spoke to Eve, it means that Adam, the head, was very much involved in this process. Think as you read this commentary below, trying to rationalize how the situation played out, with the both being there.

> Eve "was indeed deceived," but Adam "was not deceived." Of course, this cannot be taken absolutely. It must mean something on this order: Adam was not deceived in the manner in which Eve was deceived. See Gen. 3:4–6. She listened directly to Satan; he did not. She sinned before he did. She was the leader. He was the follower. She led when she should have followed; that is, she led in the way of sin, when she should have followed in the path of righteousness.[48]

The reason for the difficulty is this, they are taking it as though Adam and Eve are standing before the tree of knowledge of good and evil, and the serpent, Satan, starts to speak to Eve. They carry on a conversation, with Adam simply passively listening. Satan deceives Eve, but Adam is not deceived, yet he does not argue with the serpent, snatch the fruit from Eve, but rather just stands there letting Eve eat the fruit, knowing she will die. Really? I just cannot see how that can rationally be the case. I would argue that Eve was alone, before Adam joined her.

Was Adam standing beside Eve when she had the conversation with the serpent, was deceived and chose to rebel against God? The Bible shows no indication that this is the case. The translations above make it appear as though that is the case, "she took of its fruit and ate, and she also **gave** some to **her husband who was with her**, and he ate."

The Hebrew verb translated "gave" is in the imperfect waw consecutive, as a result, it points to a temporal or logical sequence (usually called an "imperfect sequential"). Hence, a Bible translator or committee can translate the several occurrences of the waw, which tie together the chain of events in verse 6, with "and" as well as other transitional words, such as "subsequently," "then," "after that," afterward," and "so."

---

[48] William Hendriksen and Simon J. Kistemaker, vol. 4, Exposition of the Pastoral Epistles, New Testament Commentary, 110 (Grand Rapids: Baker Book House, 1953-2001).

Genesis 3:6 English Standard Version (ESV)	**Genesis 3:6** Updated American Standard Version (UASV)
6 So when the woman saw that the tree was good for food, **and** that it was a delight to the eyes, **and** that the tree was to be desired to make one wise, she took of its fruit **and** ate, **and** she also gave some to her husband who was with her, **and** he ate.	**6** So when the woman saw that the tree was good for food, **and** that it was a delight to the eyes, **and** that the tree was to be desirable to make one wise, **and** she took of its fruit **and** ate, *then* she also gave some to her husband when with her, **and** he ate.

One has to ask themselves, would Adam have passively stood beside his wife Eve, listening to the conversation, between her and the serpent, as Satan spewed forth lies and malicious talk through this serpent, especially, especially, when Paul tells us explicitly that he was not deceived by the serpent? Supposedly, Adam just stood there and remained silent? Adam just chose not to interrupt the peddling of lies. Listen to the Bible scholar below, he actually believes this is reasonable.

> Genesis 3:6 makes it clear that he was "with her" during the interchange with the serpent, but he remained silent. He should have interrupted. He should have chased the serpent off. And when it comes down to it, when he is offered the fruit himself, he eats it--no questions asked, no protests given. Adam and Eve together rebelled against their Creator, so they both suffer the horrible consequences.[49]

The conversation with the serpent reveals that Adam had previously carried out his responsibilities as the head, informing her of the command not to eat from the tree. (Gen. 3:3) It seems far more likely that Satan, through the serpent ignored this headship, going after the newer person in the Garden of Eden, Eve, when she was alone. Eve later replied, "The serpent deceived me, and I ate."

Let us assume that I am simply mistaken, and it should be translated, "and she also gave some to her husband who was with her." Adam need not be clear on the other side of the Garden; he could have just been out of hearing range, and still have been with her. Suppose he was across the field, visually in sight, but still out of hearing range, it could still be said he was with her. Husbands have you ever been in a huge store with your wife, like Wal-Mart, and at the same time you are on one side of the

---

[49] Longman III, Tremper (2005-05-12). How to Read Genesis (How to Read Series How to Read) (p. 111). Intervarsity Press - A. Kindle Edition.

store (lawn-garden or automotive), and she is on the other side of the store. If you were to say you were **with your wife** at Wal-Mart, would that mean that you were necessarily standing right beside her. Say an issue came up in the store, so you walked over. The Garden of Eden was no small place, like a city park, but more like the size of a state park, possibly 18,000 acres of land and 3,000 acres of water. If Adam were in eyesight, but out of hearing range, it could still be said that he was with her. She could have called him over after her transgression, at which point, he demonstrated that his love for her was greater than that of his Creator, and so he ate.

Genesis 3:8 Did God speak directly to Adam?

Generally, in the Bible, when God had dealings with the human family, it was by means of an angel. (Genesis 16:7-11; 18:1-3, 22-26; 19:1; Judges 2:1-4; 6:11-16, 22; 13:15-22) The primary person in Scripture, who spoke and had dealings with humans, as a representative of the Father, Jehovah God, was his only only-begotten Son, appropriately called "the Word." (John 1:1) Therefore, while the Bible does not explicitly say, it was very likely that God spoke with Adam and Eve by means of "the Word." Genesis 1:26-28; 2:16; 3:8-13.

Genesis 3:17 How is it that the ground would be cursed for Adam, and for how long?

The curse that Jehovah God had placed on the ground meant that cultivation was going to be a far greater task than it would have been had Adam not sinned. Lamech, Noah's father, in connection with the thorns and thistles, expresses this level of the curse, "the painful toil of our hands." (Gen 5:29) The curse was lifted after the flood, at which time God blessed his faithful servants Noah and his sons. (Gen 9:1) Jehovah gave Noah and his family a good start, reissued the command to multiply and fill the earth (Gen 13:10), and placed under man's power the animal and plant realms, with no handicapping curse on the earth: "I will never again curse the soil because of man." However, take note that the work of cultivating the entire earth given to Adam was not contained within that given to Noah. This suggests that there would not be an earth wide paradise accomplished by imperfect man, just because the curse was lifted. (Gen. 1:28; 6:17; 8:21; 9:1-17)

Genesis 3:19-21 Will Adam and Eve be among those receiving a resurrection?

The conclusion below will be drawn from silence, and cannot be taken dogmatically. It is inferential only, and the final answer will have to be one that we seldom like, 'we will have to wait and see.' However, just because something is drawn from silence does not necessarily mean it is not true. We have absolutely no record that Jesus ever bathed, but we can be most certain that he did. It is certainly true that both Adam and Eve attempted to sidestep their responsibility of eating from the forbidden tree. Adam blamed Eve, while Eve blamed the serpent. However, both did not deny that they had actually violated the command.

Jehovah has said that if you eat from this tree, "you shall surely die." (Gen 2:17) That was the explicit punishment, death. There sentence was to "suffer the punishment of eternal destruction." (2 Thess 1:9) The reason that this could be said is, justice required death, with no provision for anything else at the time that they were given the command. It does not seem fair that a Just God, in his command, would not include additional punishments of Eve's difficulty in childbirth and Adam's struggle to get the earth to respond to his care, if they were a part of the original provision. It seems that the extra penalty for Eve ("I will greatly multiply thy pain and thy conception; in pain thou shalt bring forth children"), and for Adam ("cursed is the ground for thy sake; in toil shalt thou eat of it all the days of thy life"); where a means to move the two to repentance. Do the extra penalties, which were not part of the original punishment, for eating the forbidden fruit, mean that Jehovah was going to forgive them after they paid the price that he had laid down? The Apostle Paul said at Romans 6:7, "he that hath died is justified from sin."

Just as humankind are under the condemnation of death, because we are sinners; as Romans 5:12 informs us, "therefore, as through one man sin entered into the world, and death through sin; and so death passed unto all men, for that all sinned." Thus, it would seem that Adam and Eve could be afforded this as well, being chastised beyond the original punishment, because of Jehovah's love for them. In fact, he did not give them this additional punishment, until after he informed them of the hope held out to all of humankind, the hope of a coming seed. (Gen 3:15) Discipline by God is because of his love, and it always starts as a means of correction, this extra chastisement was a constructive reminder of their unfaithfulness to him and their need to return and repent. We have no knowledge that they ever returned to God, or that they did not for that matter.

It is very much possible that when Jehovah God clothed and protected the first human couple, he informed them, of the coming seed, Jesus Christ (Gen 3:15), who would crush the head of the serpent (Satan), and "give his life as a ransom for many." (Matt 20:28) It would seem that God must have informed Adam of the atoning value of the blood sacrifice as well. Otherwise, we are in a difficulty, as to how Abel, Adam's second son, acquired this knowledge. (Gen 4:4)

Both Cain and Abel brought their offering to the altar individually. This means that Adam had no priestly function. The vegetable offering of Cain would have been displeasing to Adam, because it was displeasing to Jehovah. Cain's offering lacked the atoning blood. (Gen 4:5) On the other hand, Jehovah was well pleased with Abel's blood atoning sacrifice of "the firstborn of his flock and of their fat portions." (Gen 4:4)

Some may argue that Adam and Eve were perfect, and this would indicate that they had no excuse for their rebellious act, which means that they willfully and knowingly sinned against God under perfection, like the blasphemy against the "Spirit" that Jesus spoke of, forfeiting any hope of a resurrection. (Matt 12:32; Heb. 6:4-6) They would point out maybe that we in our imperfection are prone, inclined, leaned toward sin, while Adam and Eve were prone, inclined and leaned toward good. However, the Christian can find himself, because of the ransom sacrifice of Christ, in an approved standing before God. There are allowances made for his imperfection, which means, he has a righteous standing before God. (Ps 103:8-14) Thus, if we were to put them on a scale, Adam would not have needed any allowance for his standing before Jehovah, while God graciously gives imperfect man that exercises faith in Christ some counter weights undeservedly so, to offset and give him his standing before Jehovah.

In the end, we must say that there is no conclusive answer to this question. One should offer both arguments, and allow the listener to decide for themselves where they stand. The other option is to be neutral and not commit to either position, choosing to wait and see, as God is a God of mercy, love and justice, and will do the right thing. In conclusion, it is difficult for this writer to believe that Adam and Eve spent 930 years and did not repair their relationship with their Father.

Genesis 3:24 Was God the inventor of swords?

After Adam and Eve sinned and were ejected from the garden, Jehovah banned them from returning. How? Genesis 3:24 says: "So he drove the man out, and placed cherubim east of the garden of Eden, and a flaming, turning sword to guard the way to the tree of life." Notice, "a flaming, turning sword." Was Jehovah God the inventor of swords?

The idea that the God that we know as being the epitome of love, while at the same time, being the inventor of what we know as the sword, is not a necessary logical conclusion. All Adam and Eve saw turning in front of the angel that was guarding the entrance to the Garden of Eden was a blazing object. What it was specifically, we do not know. At the time Moses penned Genesis, the sword was a common weapon of warfare, and as a means of defending oneself. (Genesis 31:26; 34:26; 48:22; Exodus 5:21; 17:13) Therefore, Moses' words "a flaming, turning sword" allowed his readers to visualize to a certain point what existed at the entrance of the Garden of Eden. We have a common saying today that 'a picture is worth a thousand words,' which is certainly true, and would have been no less true for Bible writers. By Moses giving a visual aid, he would have helped his readers better appreciate and have a better understanding.

Genesis 3:24 Why Has God Permitted Wickedness and Suffering?

Agnostic Bible scholar Dr. Bar D. Ehrman includes a Question and Answer section at the end of his book, Misquoting Jesus, in which he is asked about "*What big question(s) would have to be answered to your satisfaction for you to return to the Christian faith or some form of religious observance?*"

> The big issue that drove me to Agnosticism [Ehrman is now an Atheist] has to do not with the Bible, but with the pain and suffering in the world. I eventually found it impossible to explain the evil so rampant among us—whether in terms of genocides (which continue), unspeakable human cruelty, war disease, hurricanes, tsunamis, mudslides, the starvation of millions of innocent children, you name it—if there was a good and loving God who was actively involved in this world.
> **Misquoting Jesus (p. 248)**

As you will see with this chapter and the next, Ehrman's issue is simply a matter of starting with the wrong premise. Point One: He starts with 'if God is a God of love, who has the power to fix anything, how can there have been such horrific pain and suffering in imperfection over the last 6,000 years?' Point Two: He also likely starts with the premise that 'God is responsible for everything that happens.' If one starts with the wrong premise, there is no doubt that he will reach the wrong conclusion(s). Point One is dealt with below, but let it be said that Ehrman is looking through the binoculars from the wrong end, the big side through the small. When you do that, you get a narrow, focused outlook. God looks through the binoculars the right way, and can see the big picture. Ehrman can only see but a fraction and a moment of time, 70 – 80 years, while God sees everything that has happen these past 6,000 plus years in the greatest of detail, and can see what the outcome would be if he had handled things in a variety of ways.

Point Two is certainly one reason suffering and evil is often misunderstood. God is responsible for everything, but not always directly. If he started the human race, and we end up with what we now have, in essence, he is responsible. Just as parents, who have a child are similarly responsible for the child committing murder 21 years into his life, because they procreated and gave birth to the child. The mother and father are **in**directly responsible. King David commits adultery with Bathsheba and has her husband Uriah killed to cover things up, and impregnates Bathsheba, but the adulterine child, who remains nameless, died. Is God responsible for the death of that child? We can answer yes and no to that question. He is responsible in two ways: **(1)** He created humankind, so there would have been no affair, murder, adulterine child if he had not. **(2)** He did not step in and save the child, when he had the power to do so. However, he is not directly responsible, because he did not make King David and Bathsheba commit the acts that led to the child being born, nor did he bring an illness on the adulterine child, he just did not step in to save the child, in a time that had a high rate of infant deaths.

The reason why people think that God does not care about us is the words of religious leaders, which have made them, feel this way. When a tragedy strikes, what do pastors and Bible scholars often say? When 9/11 took place, with thousands dying in the twin towers of New York, many ministers said: "It was God's will. God must have had some good reason for doing this." When religious leaders make such comments or similar ones, they are actually blaming God for the bad things that happen. Yet, the disciple James wrote, "Let no one say when he is tempted, 'I am being tempted by God,' for God cannot be tempted with evil, and he himself tempts no one." (James 1:13) God never directly causes what is bad. Indeed, "far be it from God that he should do wickedness, and from the Almighty that he should do wrong."—Job 34:10.

The history of humans has been inundated with pain and suffering on an unprecedented scale, much of which they have brought on themselves. The question that has plagued many a person is, 'why if there is a loving God, would he allow it to start with, and worse still, why allow it to go on for over 6,000 years?' Many apologist scholars have struggled to answer this question, because they are over analyzing, as opposed to just looking for the answer in God's Word. Therefore, if we are to answer this question, we must go back to Adam and Eve at the time of the first sin. Many have read this account, but I will list the texts as a refresher.

Genesis 2:17 Update American Standard Version (UASV)

17 but from the tree of the knowledge of good and evil you shall not eat,**50** for in the day that you eat from it you shall surely die."**51**

As you can see, humankind's continued existence in a paradise, with perfection, was dependent upon obedience, his continued acceptance of God as his sovereign.

Genesis 3:1-5 Update American Standard Version (UASV)

1 Now the serpent was more crafty than any beast of the field which Jehovah God had made. And he said to the woman, "Did God actually say, 'You**52** shall not eat of any tree in the garden'?" **2** And the woman said to the serpent, "From the fruit of the trees of the garden we may eat, **3** but from the tree that is in the midst of the garden, God said, 'You shall not eat from it, nor shall you touch it, lest you die'." **4** And the serpent said to the woman, "You shall not surely die. **5** For God knows that when you eat of it your eyes will be opened, and you will be like God, knowing good and evil." knowing good and evil.

Later Bible texts establish Satan the Devil as the one using a serpent as his mouthpiece, like a ventriloquist would a dummy. Anyway, take note that Satan contradicts the clear statement made to Adam at Genesis 2:17, "you will not surely die." Backing up a little, we see Satan asking an

---

[50] Lit *eat from it*

[51] Lit *dying you* [singular] *shall die.* Heb *moth tamuth*; the first reference to death in the Scriptures

[52] In Hebrew *you* is plural in verses 1–5

inferential question, "Did God actually say, 'You shall not eat of any tree in the garden'?" First, he is overstating what he knows to be true, not "any tree," just one tree. Second, Satan is inferring, 'I can't believe that God would say . . . how dare he say such.' Notice too that Eve has been told so thoroughly about the tree that she even goes beyond what Adam told her, not just that you 'do not eat from it,' no, 'you do not even touch it!' Then, Satan out and out lied and slandered God as a liar, saying that 'they would not die.' To make matters much worse, he infers that God is withholding good from them, and by rebelling they would be better off, being like God, 'knowing good and bad.' This latter point is not knowledge of; it is the self-sovereignty of choosing good and bad for oneself, and created creatures acting in a rebellious manner. What was symbolized by the tree is well expressed in a footnote on Genesis 2:17, in The Jerusalem Bible (1966):

> This knowledge is a privilege which God reserves to himself and which man, by sinning, is to lay hands on, 3:5, 22. Hence it does not mean omniscience, which fallen man does not possess; nor is it moral discrimination, for unfallen man already had it and God could not refuse it to a rational being. It is the power of deciding for himself what is good and what is evil and of acting accordingly, a claim to complete moral independence by which man refuses to recognize his status as a created being. The first sin was an attack on God's sovereignty, a sin of pride.

The Issues at Hand

(1) Satan called God a liar and said he was not to be trusted, as to the life or death issue.

(2) Satan's challenge therefore took into question the right and legitimacy of God's rightful place as the Universal Sovereign.

(3) Satan also suggested that people would remain obedient to God only as long as their submission to God was to their benefit.

(4) Satan all but said that humankind was able to walk on its own, there being no need for dependence on God.

(5) Satan argued that man could be like God, choosing for himself what is right and wrong.

(6) Satan claimed that God's way of ruling was not in the best interests of humans, and they could do better without God.

Job 1:6-11 Update American Standard Version (UASV)

6 Now there was a day when the sons of God came to present themselves before Jehovah, and Satan also came among them. **7** Jehovah said to Satan, "From where do you come?" Then Satan answered Jehovah and said, "From roaming about on the earth and walking around on it." **8** Jehovah said to Satan, "Have you considered my servant Job? For there is no one like him on the earth, a blameless and upright man, fearing God and turning away from evil." **9** Then Satan answered Jehovah, "<u>Does Job fear God for nothing</u>? **10** Have you not made a hedge about him and his house and all that he has, on every side? You have blessed the work of his hands, and his possessions have increased in the land. **11** But put forth your hand now and <u>touch all that he has; he will surely curse you to your face</u>."

Job 2:4-5 Update American Standard Version (UASV)

4 Satan answered Jehovah and said, "Skin for skin! Yes, all that <u>a man</u> has he will give for his life. **5** However, put forth your hand now, and touch his bone and his flesh; he will curse you to your face."

This general reference to "a man," as opposed to specifically naming Job, is suggesting that all men [and women] will only obey God when things are good, but when the slightest difficulty arises, he will not obey. If you were put to the test, would you prove your love for your heavenly Father and show that you preferred His rule to that of any other?

God Settles the Issues

There is one thing that Satan did not challenge—the power of God. Satan did not suggest that God was unable to destroy him as an accuser of God's creatures. However, he did challenge God's way of ruling, not His right to rule. Therefore, it is a moral issue that must be settled.

An illustration of how God chose to deal with the issue can be demonstrated in human terms. A neighbor down the street slandered a man, who had a son and a daughter. The slanderer said that he was not a good father, that he withheld good from his children, and was so overbearing, to the point of being abusive. The slanderer stated that the children would be better off without the father. He further argued that the children had no real love for their father, and only obeyed him because of the food and shelter. How should the father deal with these false and slanderous accusations? If he were to go down the street and pummel the slanderer, it would only validate the lies, making the neighbors believe he is telling the truth.

The answer lies within his family, they can serve only as his witnesses. (Pro 27:11; Isa 43:10) If the children stay obedient and grow to be successful adults, turning out to be loving, caring, honest people with spotless character, it proves the accusations were false. If the children accept the lies, and rebel, and grow up to be despicable people, it just further validates that they would have been better off by staying with the father. This is how God chose to deal with the issues. The issues that were raised must be settled beyond all reasonable doubt.

If God had destroyed the rebellious three: Satan, Adam and Eve; he would have not resolved the issues of whether man could walk on his own, if he would be better off without his Creator, if God's rulership was not best, and if God were hiding good from man. In addition, there was an audience of untold billions of angelic spirit creatures looking on. If God destroyed without settling things, these spirit persons would be following God out of dreadful fear, not love, fear of displeasing God. Moreover, say He did destroy them, and start over, and ten thousand years down the road (with billions of humans now on earth), the issues were raised again, He would have to destroy billions of people again, and again, and again all throughout time, until these issues were laid to rest.

What God has done is to allow time to pass, and the issues to be resolved. Man thought he was better off without God, and could walk on his own. In addition, man has attempted every kind of rulership imaginable, and one must ask, 'have they proven themselves better than rulership under the sovereignty of their Creator?' (Proverbs 1:30-33; Isaiah 59:4, 8) Sadly, the issues must be taken up to the brink of destroying man (Rev 11:18), otherwise, the argument would be that if given enough time, they could have turned things around. If man goes up to the point of destroying himself and Armageddon comes at the last minute, it will have set a case law, solved the issue, and the Bible can serve as the example forever. If the issues of God's sovereignty or the loyalty of His created creatures, angelic or human, is ever questioned again, we would have the Holy Bible that will serve as a law established based on previous verdicts of not guilty, please see below.

What Have the Results Been?

(1) God does not cause evil and suffering. He does not cause injustices. Romans 9:14.

(2) That fact that God has allowed evil, pain and suffering has proved that independence from God has not brought about a better world. Jeremiah 8:5, 6, 9.

(3) God's permission of evil, pain and suffering has also proved that Satan has not been able to turn all humans away from God. Exodus 9:16; 1 Samuel 12:22; Hebrews 12:1.

(4) The fact that God has permitted evil, pain and suffering to continue has provided proof that only God, the Creator, has the capability and the right to rule over humankind for their eternal blessing and happiness. Ecclesiastes 8:9.

(5) Satan has been the god of this world since the sin in Eden (over 6,000 years), and how has that worked out for man, and what has been the result of man's course of independence from God and his rule? Matthew 4:8-9; John 16:11; 2 Corinthians 4:3-4; 1 John 5:19; Psalm 127:1.

Satan's impact on the earth's activities has carried with it conflict, evil and death, and his rulership has been by means of deception, power and his own self-interest. He has demonstrated himself an unfit ruler of everything. Therefore, God is now completely vindicated in putting an end to this corrupted rebel along with all who have shared in his evil deeds. (Romans 16:20)

God has tolerated evil, sickness, pain, suffering and death until our day in order to resolve all the issues raised by Satan. We are self-centered in thinking that this has only pained us. Imagine that you are holding a rope on a sinking ship that 20 other men, women and children are clinging to, when your child loses her grip and falls into the ocean. You can either hold the rope, saving 20 people, or you can let go and attempt to rescue your daughter. God has been watching the suffering of billions from the day of Adam and Eve's sin. Moreover, it has been His great love for us, which causes Him to cling to the rope of issues, saving us from a future of repeated issues. Nevertheless, he will not allow this evil to remain forever. He has set a fixed time (Acts 17.31) when He will end this wicked system of Satan's rule.

Daniel 11:27 Update American Standard Version (UASV)

27 As for both kings, their heart will be inclined to do what is evil, and they will speak lies to each other at the same table; but it will not succeed, for the end is still to come at the appointed time.

Unlike what many people of the world may think (the world that lies in the hands of Satan), being obedient to God is not difficult. We simply must set our pride aside and accept that the wisdom of God is so far greater than our own, and accept that He has worked for the good of obedient humankind, as He loves each one of us.

Matthew 7:21 Update American Standard Version (UASV)

21 "Not everyone who says to me, 'Lord, Lord,' will enter the kingdom of heaven, but the one who does the will of my Father who is in heaven.

1 John 2:15-17 Update American Standard Version (UASV)

15 Do not love the world or the things in the world. If anyone loves the world, the love of the Father is not in him. **16** For all that is in the world, the lust of the flesh and the lust of the eyes and the boastful pride of life, is not from the Father, but is from the world. **17** The world is passing away, and its lusts; but the one who does the will of God remains forever.

As Christians, there is a love we must not have. We must 'not love the world or anything in it.' Instead, we need to keep from becoming infected by the corruption of unrighteous human society that is alienated from God and must not breathe in its mental disposition or be moved by its sinful dominant attitude. (Ephesians 2:1, 2; James 1:27) If we were to have the views of those in the world that are in opposition to God, "the love of the Father" would not be in us. (James 4:4)

Genesis 4:3 Why was Cain's offering unacceptable to God?

There are two aspects of Cain's offering, which found him unapproved before God: **(1)** his attitude and **(2)** the type of offering.

Eventually, Cain and Abel came before God with their offerings. "Cain brought of the fruit of the ground an offering to Jehovah." (Gen 4:3, ASV) "Abel also brought of the firstborn of his flock and of their fat portions."[53] (Gen 4:4, ESV) It is likely that both Cain and Abel were close

---

[53] 4:4–5 Abel's offering was acceptable (cf. Heb. 11:4), not just because it was an animal, nor just because it was the very best of what he had, nor even that it was the culmination of a zealous heart for God, but because it was in every way obediently given according to what God must have revealed (though not recorded in Genesis). Cain, disdaining the divine instruction, just brought what he wanted to bring: some of his crop.– MacArthur, John (2005-05-09). *The MacArthur Bible Commentary* (Kindle Locations 2161-2163). Thomas Nelson. Kindle Edition.

to 100 years old at the time, as Adam was 130 years old when he fathered his third son, Seth. (Gen 4:25; 5:3)

We can establish that the two sons became aware of their sinful state, and sought our God's favor. How they garnered this knowledge is guesswork, but it is likely by way of the father, Adam. Adam likely informed them about the coming seed and the hope that lie before humankind.[54] Therefore, it seems that they had given some thought to their condition and stand before God, and realized that they needed to try to atone for their sinful condition. The Bible does not inform us just how much time they had given to this need before they started to offer a sacrifice. Rather, God chose to convey the more important aspect, each one's heart attitude, which gives us an inside look at their thinking.

Some scholars have suggested that Eve felt that Cain was the "seed" of the Genesis 3:15 prophecy that would destroy the serpent, "she conceived and bore Cain, saying, 'I have gotten a man with the help of the LORD.'" (Gen 4:1) It might be that Cain shared in this belief and had begun to think too much of himself, and thus the haughty spirit. If this is the case, he was very mistaken. His brother Abel had a whole other spirit, as he offered his sacrifice in faith, "By faith Abel offered to God a more acceptable sacrifice than Cain, through which he was commended as righteous, God commending him by accepting his gifts." (Heb. 11:4)

It seems that Abel was capable of discerning the need for blood to be involved in the atoning sacrifice, while Cain was not, or simply did not care. Therefore, it was the heart attitude of Cain as well. Consequently, "but on Cain and his offering he did not look with favor. So Cain was very angry, and his face was downcast." (Gen 4:5, NIV) It may well be that Cain had little regard for the atoning sacrifice, giving it little thought, going through the motions of the act only. However, as later biblical history would show, Jehovah God is not one to be satisfied with formal worship. Cain had developed a bad heart attitude, and Jehovah well knew that his motives were not sincere. The way Cain reacted to the evaluation of his sacrifice only evidenced what Jehovah already knew. Instead of seeking to improve the situation, "Cain was very angry, and his face was downcast." (Gen 4:5) As you read the rest of the account, it will

---

[54] Adam's family must have received God's revelation about the necessity of sacrifice to create and maintain fellowship with God. The background to this was probably the sacrifice that God performed to provide the clothing to cover Adam and Eve's shame (see Gen. 3:21). Anders, Max; Gangel, Kenneth; Bramer, Stephen J. (2003-04-01). Holman Old Testament Commentary - Genesis: 1 (p. 56). Holman Reference. Kindle Edition.

become clearer as to the type of temperament Cain had before Jehovah God.

Genesis 4:6-16 Updated American Standard Version (USV)

6 Then Jehovah said to Cain, "Why are you angry, and why has your face fallen? **7** If you do well, will there not be a lifting up?[55] And if you do not do well, sin is crouching at the door. Its desire is for you, but you must rule over it."

8 Cain said to Abel his brother. And it came about when they were in the field, that Cain rose up against Abel his brother and killed him.

9 Then Jehovah[56] said to Cain, "Where is Abel your brother?" And he said, "I do not know. Am I my brother's keeper?" **10** He said, "What have you done? The voice of your brother's blood is crying to me from the ground. **11** Now you are cursed from the ground, which has opened its mouth to receive your brother's blood from your hand. **12** When you cultivate the ground, it will no longer yield its strength to you; you will be a fugitive and a wanderer on the earth." **13** Cain said to Jehovah, "My punishment is greater than I can bear! **14** Behold, you have driven me today away from the ground, and from your face I shall be hidden. I shall be a fugitive and a wanderer on the earth, and whoever finds me will kill me." **15** So Jehovah said to him, "Therefore whoever kills Cain, vengeance will be taken on him sevenfold." And Jehovah put a mark on Cain, so that no one finding him would slay him.

16 Then Cain went out from the presence of Jehovah, and dwelt in the land of Nod,[57] east of Eden.

Genesis 4:5 Does God not have respect for mankind?

Genesis 4:5 King James Version (KJV)

[5]But unto Cain and to his offering he had not respect. And Cain was very wroth,[58] and his countenance[59] fell.

---

[55] This is a shortening of the Hebrew idiom "to lift up the face," which means "to accept" favorably

[56] The Tetragrammaton, God's personal name, יהוה (JHVH/YHWH), which is found in the Hebrew Old Testament 6,828 times.

[57] I.e. wandering

Romans 2:11 King James Version (KJV)

[11]For there is no respect of persons with God.

Deuteronomy 10:17 King James Version (KJV)

[17]For the LORD your God is God of gods, and Lord of lords, a great God, a mighty, and a terrible, which regardeth not persons, nor taketh reward:

First, it is immediately obvious from Scripture that we were created in the image of God, and even in our imperfection, we carry a measure of that. Therefore, God does have respect for his creation, to do otherwise would be to disrespect himself.

Second, we need to appreciate that literal translations can be a little more difficult to understand, and this is actually a good thing, because it causes us to pause and ponder.

Third, you will find as we work our way through this publication that the King James Version has been improved upon, and many of the Bible difficulties will be better understood by simply looking to a modern literal translation. If you look at Deuteronomy 10:17 in the King James Version, it reads that God, "regardeth no persons." This can be better grasped by looking at the English Standard Version, which reads, "God, who is not partial." Moses is telling his readers that God is not partial in his justice that he meets out to man. In other words, as the text goes on to say, he "takes no bribe."

However, it is the type of person that Jehovah God has no respect for, such as Cain, who slew his brother, because he had a wicked heart. Moreover, he lacked respect for Cain even prior to that, because Cain lacked faith when he came before Jehovah with his offering. (Heb. 11:4)

At Malachi 1:2-3 God says, "I loved Jacob," then he states, "Esau I have hated." What brought on this contrast between these two brothers? First, it must be noted, this "love" and "hate" contrast in the Bible is understood to mean, not that he literally "hated," but that he loved less. Even still, it is the fact that Jacob loved God and magnified him, while Esau failed to do so. Genesis 25:34 tells the reader "Esau despised his

---

[58] 4:5–6 very angry. Rather than being repentant for his sinful disobedience, Cain was violently hostile toward God, whom he could not kill, and jealous of his brother, whom he could kill (cf. 1 John 3:12; Jude 11).–MacArthur, John (2005-05-09). *The MacArthur Bible Commentary* (Kindle Locations 2164-2166). Thomas Nelson. Kindle Edition.

[59] a person's face or facial expression

birthright." It is not that Jehovah hates the person; it is their willfulness sinning and practice of sin that he hates.

Genesis 4:7 Why would the language, 'sin is crouching at the door, its desire is for you,' be used if before the Flood, animals ate only vegetation?

God warned Cain that 'sin is crouching at the door, and its desire is for you,' which appears to refer to a wild beast and its prey. (Genesis 4:7) If animals only age vegetation before the flood, why would that language be used?

First, one interpretation principle is to never expect more out of a book than its intended purpose. The was not written to be a science textbook, a history book, a book on geography, yet it touches on these subjects in passing along the message that Jehovah God want mankind to receive. In Genesis, there are a number of verses that reveal facts or historical information that might seem oddly out of place in their historical setting. Please see other examples of Moses informing his readers by updating the information (Gen 2:10-14), or using visual aids (Gen 3:24)

At Genesis 4:7 God warned Cain: "If you do well will I not accept you? But if you do not do well, sin is crouching at the door. And its desire is for you, but you must rule over it." The language appears to depict the image of a hungry wild beast crouched to jump on and devour prey.

Nevertheless, The Bible seems to indicate that Adam and Eve were at peace with all the animals, and had no reason to fear them. It is quite possible that some of the animals were more comfortable around them than others; while others were wild beats that dwelt outside of the human family. (Genesis 1:25, 30; 2:19) However, the Bible seems to be quite clear that none of the animals preyed upon the other animals, or humans. In the beginning, God precisely assigned vegetation as the food for both animals and humans. (Genesis 1:29, 30; 7:14-16) There is no indication of a change in this until after the Flood, as Genesis 9:2-5 indicates.

How then are we to explain God's warning to Cain, as we read at Genesis 4:7? Surely, the visual of a vicious beast crouched and ready to jump on prey would have been effortlessly understood in Moses' day, as well as for generations thereafter, and we also understand it. Here, again, we see Moses using language adjusted to readers familiar with the post-

Flood world. While it is quite likely that Cain never saw such a creature in such a position, the point of a desire consuming him, like the wild animals that roamed outside of the human population, would have not been misunderstood.

Our focus on the text should not be like the Bible critic, who looks for chinks in the armor, but to appreciate that the Creator of all things, was very kind in giving Cain a warning, and our need to not be like Cain, but to humbly accept the counsel from God's Word. We do not want to allow jealousy to corrupt and of our relationships. Moreover, we need to heed the divine warnings that we find within Scripture. Exodus 18:20; Ecclesiastes 12:12; Ezekiel 3:17-21; 1 Corinthians 10:11; Hebrews 12:11; James 1:14, 15; Jude 7, 11.

Genesis 4:12-13 Why did Cain not receive capital punishment for the murder he committed?

Genesis 9:6 Updated American Standard Version (USV)

6 " Whoever sheds man's blood,
By man his blood shall be shed,
For in the image of God
he made man.

Exodus 21:12 Updated American Standard Version (USV)

12 "He who strikes a man so that he dies shall be put to death.

As can be seen from the above, the penalty for willfully taking the life of another is the death penalty. We see from the account concerning Cain that he not only did not receive the death penalty for murdering his brother Abel, but he was given protection from anyone seeking to avenge that murder. (Gen 4:15)

At first glance, this may seem like a inconsistency on the part of Jehovah's justice, but it is not. There are multiple reasons as to why Cain did not receive the death penalty. At the time of this murder, God had not established the death penalty for the murder of another. (Rom 13:1-4) It was only after, "the LORD saw that the wickedness of man was great in the earth, and that every intention of the thoughts of his heart was only evil continually." (Gen 6:5) After the destruction of the Nephilim and wicked man by means of the flood, did God say, ""Whoever sheds the blood of man, by man shall his blood be shed . . ." (Gen 9:6)

Jehovah is the giver of life and death, and he rightly chose to give Cain a life sentence of banishment. (Deut. 32:39) However, God did express his thoughts that Cain was worthy of death. Jehovah said, "What have you done? The voice of your brother's blood is crying to me from the ground." (Gen 4:10) Even Cain himself knew that death was the possibility, and asked Jehovah for protection. Cain said to the Jehovah, "My punishment is greater than I can bear. Behold, you have driven me today away from the ground, and from your face I shall be hidden. I shall be a fugitive and a wanderer on the earth, and whoever finds me will kill me." (Gen 4:13-14) In addition, the death penalty then was made known as an option, for the taking of a life, as Jehovah said, "If anyone kills Cain, vengeance shall be taken on him sevenfold." (Gen 4:15) Therefore, due to mitigating circumstances, Cain is the exception to the rule, and cannot be used against the justice of the death penalty that was to become a part of human law after the flood.

Genesis 4:15 How did God "put a mark on Cain"?

The Bible does not say exactly what this mark was, but it is highly unlikely that it was a physical mark on his person. Such a mark would be meaningless centuries later when thousands of people were living before the flood. The sign was likely a verbal decree made by Jehovah to Adam and Eve, which would have become an oral tradition that would have been passed down from generation to generation, avoiding the murder of Cain for the sake of revenge.

Genesis 4:17 Where did Cain get his wife?

Genesis 4:17 Updated American Standard Version (UASV)

[17] Cain had sexual relations[60] with his wife and she conceived, and gave birth to Enoch; and he built a city, and called the name of the city Enoch, after the name of his son, Enoch.

Genesis 3:20 Updated American Standard Version (UASV)

[20] Now the man called his wife's name Eve,[61] because she was the mother of all living.

---

[60] Lit knew

[61] 3:20. In Genesis 2:23 Adam declared that his wife would "be called 'woman,' for she was taken out of man." Now, after the fall, and hearing the elements of judgment,

Here we are just setting up the situation, and as you can see, all humans came to be the offspring of Adam and Eve.

Genesis 5:3-4 Updated American Standard Version (UASV)

3 When Adam had lived one hundred and thirty years, he became[62] the father of a son in his own likeness, according to his image, and named him Seth. 4 Then the days of Adam after he became the father of Seth were eight hundred years, and he had other sons and daughters.

As you can see, aside from Cain and Abel, there was Seth, as well as "other sons and daughters." Therefore, one of Adam's daughters must have married Cain. In fact, they lived for centuries; it could have even been a niece. We must keep in mind that these are the immediate descendants of Adam and Eve; therefore, they would have been closer to perfection. Their condition of good health would be far beyond the healthiest person living today; so, there would have been no chance of passing on defects, as would be the case even in the Time of Abraham, when they were still living almost 200 years. This is reason you find Jehovah God forbidding incest 2.500 years later in the Mosaic Law.

Genesis 4:16-17 Updated American Standard Version (UASV)

16 Then Cain went out from the presence of Jehovah, and dwelt in the land of Nod,[63] east of Eden.

17 Cain had sexual relations[64] with his wife and she conceived, and gave birth to Enoch; and he built a city, and called the name of the city Enoch, after the name of his son, Enoch.

Please note that Cain met his wife before he fled to another land. She was not from some other family. However, it was there that they had relations, and fathered a son.

Adam named the woman Eve. This verse should be seen as indication of Adam's acceptance of and faith in God's decrees that had just been given. The name Eve means "living" or "life producer." By the personal name he gave his wife, Adam declared that he believed she would conceive and produce offspring for she would become the mother of all the living. He accepted God's judgments but believed God's word about children and perhaps implicitly proclaimed his faith that some day an offspring of his would conquer the Evil One.—Anders, Max; Gangel, Kenneth; Bramer, Stephen J. (2003-04-01). Holman Old Testament Commentary - Genesis: 1 (p. 46). B&H Publishing. Kindle Edition.

62 Lit *begot*

63 I.e. wandering

64 Lit *knew*

Genesis 4:26 Exactly when did the worship of God begin?

It is here that we are specifically told, "Then began men to call upon the name of Jehovah." (Gen 4:26, ASV) This is in the days of Enosh, the son of Seth, the third son of Adam and Eve. However, over 105 years earlier before the birth of Enosh, you have Abel offering sacrifices to God in faithful worship. (Gen 4:3-4) Is this not a historical error? No.

Obviously, in the days of Enosh, we are not talking about calling on the name of Jehovah in faith and pure worship as Abel had done. Some Hebrew scholars have offered that it should read, "began profanely," or "then profanation began." In reference to Enosh's day, the Targum of Onkelos says, "then in his days the sons of men desisted from praying in the Name of the Lord." The Targum[65] of Jonathan says, "That was the generation in whose days they began to err, and to make themselves idols, and surnamed their idols by the Name of the Word of the Lord." Rashi an influential Jewish Bible Commentator from the twelfth century C.E. says, "Then was there profanation in calling on the Name of the Lord." Furthermore, if purity of worship was begun in the days of Enosh, instead of profanation in calling on the Name of Jehovah, what "ungodliness" did Enoch; "the seventh from Adam" have to prophesy about in Jude 14-15? It could be that men misused the name of Jehovah by applying it to themselves, or other men, approaching God through these ones in worship. Alternatively, it could be that they applied Jehovah's name on idol objects.

---

[65] The Targum is an Aramaic translation of part of the Bible.

Review Questions

- Genesis 1:10 Is the Hebrew word for "earth" the same here as is used at Genesis 1:1, and do they mean the same thing?

- Genesis 1:16 Was light created or made, and was it on the first day or the fourth?

- Genesis 1-2 Is there a Different order of creation in Genesis 2 than Genesis 1?

- Genesis 1:26 Who are the "us" and "our" of this verse

- Genesis 2:4 "God" is used in Genesis chapter 1, while chapter 2 changes to Jehovah God. Does this mean that there are two different authors?

- Genesis 2:8 Was the Garden of Eden a real historical place?

- Genesis 2:10-14 Was the mention of Assyria an inaccurate statement?

- Genesis 2:17 Why did Adam and Eve not die in the day that they ate of the fruit from the forbidden tree?

- Genesis 2:17; 3:3 What was the fruit of the tree of the knowledge of good and evil?

- Genesis 2:17; 3:3 what did the tree of the knowledge of good and evil symbolize?

- Genesis 3:5 Is man made in the image of God or does he become like God?

- Genesis 3:6 She also gave some to her husband who was with her?

- Genesis 3:8 Did God speak directly to Adam?

- Genesis 3:17 How is it that the ground would be cursed for Adam, and for how long?

- Genesis 3:19-21 Will Adam and Eve be among those receiving a resurrection?

- Genesis 3:24 Was Jehovah God the inventor of swords?

- Genesis 3:24 Why Has God Permitted Wickedness and Suffering?

- Genesis 4:3 Why was Cain's offering unacceptable to God?

- Genesis 4:5 Does God not have respect for mankind?

- Genesis 4:7 Why would the language, 'sin is crouching at the door, its desire is for you,' be used if before the Flood, animals ate only vegetation?

- Genesis 4:12-13 Why did Cain not receive capital punishment for the murder he committed?

- Genesis 4:15 How did God "put a mark on Cain"?

- Genesis 4:17 Where did Cain get his wife?

- Genesis 4:26 Exactly when did the worship of God begin?

APPENDIX A Is the earth only 6,000 to 10,000 years old? Are the creative days literally, only 24 hours long?

There are over a dozen different interpretations concerning the creative days of Genesis. Herein we will consider the main four in an effort to make our point. First, there is the *young earth view* that asserts that all physical creation was produced in just six literal 24-hour days sometime between 6,000 and 10,000 years ago. Second, there is the *day-age view* that asserts that each creative day is to be understood figuratively as creative periods of unknown durations of time. According to this view, the earth is millions of years old, and the universe is billions of years old. Third, there is the *restoration view* (gap theory) that asserts that there is a large gap of time between Genesis 1:1 and 1:2. Fourth, there is the *literary framework view* that asserts that God was not having Moses address how He created the world, nor the length of time in which to do such. This view holds that this account in Genesis one is merely a literary outline that summarizes a theology of creation. This so-called "seven day framework" is not to be understood in a literal sense of order and chronology, but is a literary device expressing God's involvement in creation and the Sabbath. All four of these views are held by different Evangelical Christian scholars, but the authors of this book set aside three of these as being contrary to Scripture and science. We will discuss the first two views listed above in more detail below. [66]

We do not believe those who hold to the young-earth view of creationism have the evidence to support their case. Actually, we do not believe they even speak in terms of evidence. Why? Most of the young-earth commentators attempt to disprove the day-age view by using many words like "possibly," "could be," "may be," and so on. Also, we do not believe they look at the evidence without theological bias. Professor Kirk Wise writes:

> I am a young-age creationist because that is my understanding of the Scripture. As I shared with my professors years ago when I was in college, if all the evidence in the universe turns against creationism, I would be the first to admit it, but I would still be a

---

66. For a more in-depth understanding of these for creative views, see Gregory A. Boyd and Paul R. Eddy, *Across the Spectrum* (Grand Rapids, Baker Academic, 2002), 50–73.

creationist because that is what the Word of God seems to indicate. Here I must stand. (Ashton, 2001)[67]

It shows theological bias when he states that no evidence will change his mind. Just as in the case of Galileo, theologians cast doubt on the Bible by ignoring scientific evidence. The Bible was not out of harmony with the truth that the earth revolves around the sun and not the other way. God's Word needed no revision. It was the Catholic Church's misinterpretation of the Bible that caused the problem. As one grows in understanding of physics, biology, and chemistry (as is also true with history, ancient languages, and manuscripts), one may need to revise conclusions derived from previous knowledge. When knowledge increases, it calls for humility to make adjustments in ones thinking.

To suggest, as do many conservative Christians, that one needs to read the Bible in a plain way (*sensus plenoir*) is quite misleading, as though one would never consider otherwise. Galileo's own words to a pupil said it well: "Even though Scripture cannot err, its interpreters and expositors can, in various ways. One of these, very serious and very frequent, would be when they always want to stop at the purely literal sense."[68] The professor argues that because Genesis chapter one was written as historical narrative, it disallows an interpretation that has millions of years involved. This is hardly the case, for he goes on to admit that other historical narratives contain imbedded material that is not to be taken literally. Moreover, it is implied that one who accepts long creative periods must also believe the Big Bang theory, and believe that fossils are millions of years old, and believe in other facets of Evolution. This is simply untrue.

Simply put, Genesis 1:1 says: "In the beginning God created the heavens and the earth." (*ESV*) This would include our home, the earth, and our solar system and galaxy that King David referred to when he looked into the night sky and wrote: "When I look at your heavens, the work of your fingers, the moon and the stars, which you have set in place, what is man that you are mindful of him, and the son of man that you care for him?" (Psalm 8:3, 4, *ESV*) It would also include all the billions of universes that David was unable to see with his naked eye. Therefore, all this came *before* the first day of creative preparation for life on the earth that starts in Genesis 1:3, as would also be the case with the description of the earth as found in verse 2. It is not until we get to

---

67. http://richarddawkins.net/articles/115.
68. Letter from Galileo to Benedetto Castelli, December 21, 1613.

Genesis 1:3–5 that Moses starts to expound on the first day of creation specifically in respect to the earth.

What does this mean? It means that regardless of how long you may feel the creative days were, verses 1 and 2 are covering things that existed prior to the start of the events described in the successive creative days. Therefore, it takes nothing away from the Bible when geologists state that the earth is four billion years old, or astronomers who have calculated the age of the universe say it is at least 14–20 billion years old. For the Christian to argue with science is only history repeating itself, as you will see before this chapter closes. Again, Genesis chapter one, verses 1, 2, are outside the events of the creative days, which are simply a summary of the steps taken to transform the condition of verse 2 into the habitable earth in which the animals and Adam and Eve were created.

Now that we have settled the controversy between science and the *erroneous* interpretations of man's tradition that the universe and earth were created in only six literal days, we should clear the air over the age and origin of the sedimentary geological strata. Many have postulated that it was formed at the time of the flood of Noah. This answer is not to be found in God's Word. Those who hold to the young-earth view (6,000–10,000 years old), work very hard to try to reconcile the geologic column and the fossils of dinosaurs and such, in which they try to overcome evidence that shows the earth is millions of years old. What is now known and acknowledged by science is that the geological record does *not* contain a series of gradual and progressive stages of fossils from one species to another. Actually, the fossil record supports the creation account in that new species appear suddenly on the scene within this geological column, having absolutely no connection with any other species. The problem with young-earth proponents is that they are unable to use this information because it will not fit with their belief that all land and sea animals were created in two 24-hour days. This is not to say that this publication accepts the idea that the sea and land animals have existed for untold hundreds of millions of years, but it does not negate that the fifth and sixth creative days were possibly many thousands of years long, having flying and sea creatures, and land animals being created throughout, as well as dinosaurs.

What exactly does the Bible reveal? It says plainly that Jehovah God is the "fountain of life." (Psalm 36:9) In other words, life did not come from nothing, and then develop gradually in some evolutionary process over billions of years. Additionally, God's Word says that everything was created according to its kind. (Genesis 1:11, 21, 24) And finally, the Bible does provide the time period of man's creation, some 6,000 years ago. On this, both archaeology and Biblical chronology are not far off from each other. Creation is clearly stated within God's Word, and can be understood in relation to the correct study and interpretation of its texts, in light of factual science, astronomy, physics, chemistry, geology, and biology. The evolutionary theory stands in opposition to the Bible and to the facts of paleontology and biology. The ideas of young-earth creationists are not supported by God's Word either, conflicting with astronomy, physics, and geology.

Back in the seventeenth century, the world-renowned scientist Galileo proved beyond any doubt that the earth was not the center of the universe, nor did the sun orbit the earth. In fact, he proved it to be the other way around (no pun intended), with the earth revolving around the sun. However, he was brought up on charges of heresy by the Catholic Church and ordered to recant his position. Why? From the viewpoint of the Catholic Church, Galileo was contradicting God's Word, the Bible. As it turned out, Galileo and science were correct and the Church was wrong, for which it issued a formal apology in 1992. However, the point we wish to make here is that in all the controversy, the Bible was never in the wrong. It was a misinterpretation on the part of the Catholic Church, and not a fault with the Bible. One will find no place in the Bible that claims the sun orbits the earth. So where would the Church get such an idea? From Ptolemy (b. about 85 C.E.), an ancient astronomer, who argued for such an idea.

A geocentric model that the earth is the center of the universe was long held by Ptolemy's predecessors like Aristotle and most of the ancient Greek philosophers. The idea of the earth being the center of the universe was held on to by the fact that the observer with his naked eye saw both the sun and moon appear to revolve around the earth each day, while the earth appeared to stand still. Now consider that the church fathers of the third to the fifth centuries C.E. were inundated by Greek thought, believing philosophical thinking was a means of interpreting God's Word. Commenting on such ones, Douglas T. Holden[69] stated, "Christian theology has become so fused with Greek philosophy that it has reared individuals who are a mixture of nine parts Greek thought to one part Christian thought." Couple this with a literal reading of some texts that should be understood figuratively and you have the makings for a conflict between the Church and the scientific world.

---

69. Douglas T. Holden, *Death Shall Have no Dominion: A New Testament Study* (Bloomington: Bethany Press, 1971), 14.

In interpretation, you may find one verse that appears to be in direct conflict with another (such as, the earth will be destroyed by fire, or, the earth will last forever). We do not automatically assume that God's original Word is wrong. We must do some investigative work: (1) Is there a scribal error? (2) Is there an error in translation? (3) Is this a case of one verse using "earth" in a literal sense, while another is using figurative language, speaking of mankind as the "earth?" This can be the case with science as well. One does not let the scientific world dictate our understanding of Scripture, but we should not be so dogmatic in the face of scientific facts that we will, like Professor Kirk Wise, set aside "all the evidence in the universe [that] turns against creationism," while still holding onto erroneous, unreasonable, and unscriptural interpretations.

We have many of conservative scholarship who still argues that the earth and all life on it were created in six literal 24-hour days. As you may know, this flatly contradicts modern-day science. Do we have another Galileo moment in time? Who is correct here, the scholars or science? One thing is for certain, there is no fault to be found in God's Word. The Bible does not explicitly say these creative days were literal 24-hour days. What many are failing to realize and quite a few refuse to accept is that, in both the Hebrew and the Greek Scriptures, the word for "day" (Heb., *yohm*; Gr., *hēmera*) is used both in a literal and in a figurative sense. Moreover, this is not a case of inerrancy. In other words, if one does not accept six literal 24 hour days, he has abandoned inerrancy. True inerrancy does not consider whether they are literal or figurative creative days, but rather is your interpretation in harmony with what the author meant by the words that he used.

These six creative days are representative of being like six successive days of a week. If we look at most modern translations, they read, "**the** first day," "**the** second day," "**the** third day," and so on. This is an error in translation and should read. "And there was evening and there was morning, **a** first day." (Gen. 1:5) There is no definite article in the Hebrew of these six creative days. It is the translators that choose to add it into their translations. (ESV, LEB, HCSB, NIV, etc.) However, the American Standard Version and the New American Standard Bible read, "And there was evening and there was morning, one day." (1:5) If we were talking about a definite period of time, generally there should be a definite article in the Hebrew, because it is written in the prose genre. It is only in Hebrew poetry that the definite article could be omitted. What we are looking at with these six creative days is simply a sequential pattern, as oppose to six literal units of definite time.

SIX CREATIVE DAYS		
DAY	**WORKS**	**GENESIS**
1	Light gradually came to be;[70] a separation between day and night	1:3–5
2	Expanse, a separation between the waters below from the waters above	1:6–8
3	Dry land appears; produces vegetation	1:9–13
4	Sources of light now become visible from earth [71]	1:14–19
5	Aquatic souls and flying creatures	1:20–23
6	Land animals; man and woman created	1:24–31

While the word "day" in Hebrew can mean a 24-hour period, clearly *yohm* and context allows for the creative days to be understood as a period of time, an age, or an era. For example, immediately after he mentions the six creative days, Moses uses the same word for "day" in a more general way, lumping *all six creative days together as one day:*

Genesis 2:4: These are the generations of the heavens and of the earth when they were created, in the day that Jehovah God made earth and heaven.

Here we are given the context of just how Moses is using *yohm*, which in this verse is referring to all six creative periods as "in the day." With this alone, it is difficult to argue that in chapter one *yohm* was being used to refer literally to a 24-hour period. Below are a few other

---

70. Many believe that God said: "Let there be light" and it immediately appeared. No, this was a gradual process, taking such an enormous amount of time that speculation would be the result of any guess. J. W. Watt's translation reflects this gradual process: "And gradually light came into existence." (*A Distinctive Translation of Genesis*) This light from our sun was spread through the dark overcast, to the point that it was not at first observable but gradually became observable through time.

71. And God said, "Let there be light," and there was light, the first day. Hebrew has different words that distinguish their source and their quality. The Hebrew word used in verse one for "light" is *ohr*, which carries the general sense. However, by the fourth "day," or creative period, the Hebrew word changes to *maohr*, which is now referring to the source of the light.

examples where *yohm* is being used in the *sense* of an extended period of time, age, or era:

Proverbs 25:13: As the cold of snow *in the time* ["day" *yohm*] of harvest, So is a faithful messenger to them that send him; For he refresheth the soul of his masters.

Isaiah 4:2 (*ASV*): *In that day* [*yohm*] shall the branch of Jehovah be beautiful and glorious, and the fruit of the land shall be excellent and comely for them that are escaped of Israel.

Zechariah 14:1 (*ASV*): Behold, *a day* [*yohm*] *of* Jehovah cometh, when thy spoil shall be divided in the midst of thee.

You will have those who cling to the 24-hour creative day by informing you that *yohm*, "day, " is used 410 times outside of Genesis with a day and number and in all cases it is to be taken literally, meaning an ordinary day. First, let us point out that there is no absolute grammatical rule in Hebrew that would make this mandatory in every case. Young-earth proponents must support their proposition with their circular argument. For the sake of an argument, let us say that their claim is true. To have "day" used with an ordinal number in 410 places outside of Genesis chapter one would not negate *yohm* being used in a different setting (like creation) with ordinal numbers and still be referring to periods of time (epochs). One must keep in mind that those uses of a *yohm* outside the creation account are used in reference to humans and a human day. Because Genesis is the only place in Scripture where periods of time can be used with ordinal numbers, there is no problem with it being the exception to the rule. No other book has the setting of the creation of heaven and earth, so to equate uses of *yohm* in totally different settings with its use in Genesis is circular reasoning, as if to say: "*Yohm* is used with ordinals in 410 occurrences outside of Genesis and they are literal, so *yohm* must be literal in Genesis because it is used with ordinal numbers." You might as well say that "*yohm* is literal with ordinal numbers because *yohm* should be literal with ordinal numbers." The young-earth proponent's argument is circular by supporting a premise with a premise instead of a conclusion.

Exodus 20:11: For in six days Jehovah made heaven and earth, the sea, and all that in them is, and rested the seventh day: wherefore Jehovah blessed the sabbath day, and hallowed it.

Is Moses, the writer of Genesis, making reference here at Exodus 20:11 to the six creative days as a representative for the weekly Sabbath, thus suggesting that the six creative days were literal 24-hour days? No, this is not so. At Genesis 2:4, the same writer uses *yohm*, "day," figuratively to refer to the six creative days of Genesis chapter one and Exodus 20:11 as a whole, starting from the gradual appearance of light on the first day (Genesis 1:3, as it would appear to an earthly observer), but does not include the earth as it lay in its prior existence, in which it is described as being "without form and void, and darkness was over the face of the deep. And the Spirit of God was hovering over the face of the waters."

Another stumbling block for those who wish to take the creation account in a literal sense of 24-hour periods is that the context is really presented as events that take long periods of time to accomplish.

Genesis 1:11, 12: And God said, Let the earth put forth grass, herbs yielding seed, and fruit-trees bearing fruit after their kind, wherein is the seed thereof, upon the earth: and it was so. [Resulting in] And the earth brought forth grass, herbs yielding seed after their kind, and trees bearing fruit, wherein is the seed thereof, after their kind: and God saw that it was good.

Obviously we are dealing with far more time than one 24-hour day would allow when speaking of grass, herbs, and fruit trees sprouting *and* growing to maturity *and* producing seed and fruit.

Genesis 2:18–20: And Jehovah God said, It is not good *that the man should be alone*; I will make him a help meet for him. And out of the ground Jehovah God formed every beast of the field, and every bird of the heavens; and brought them unto the man to see what he would call them: and whatsoever the man called every living creature, that was the name thereof. And the man gave names to all cattle, and to the birds of the heavens, and to every beast of the field; but for man there was not found a help meet for him.

At this point in the creation account it was still the sixth creative day. However as verse 27 of chapter 1 shows, it is the close of the sixth creation day. After all else had been created, after the animals had been fashioned, just before sundown of that day, "God created man in his own image, in the image of God he created him; male and female he created them." Taken literally, this means that Adam and Eve were created in the last hour of the sixth day. The question here is, if the sixth "day" was only going to be 24 hours, why would Adam be lonely? God would have known he was creating his helper in that sixth "day." Why the concern for loneliness if it were only moments before Eve was to be created? For this reader, the implication is that the sixth day is a long creative period.

Even more activity would be impossibly crammed into the sixth creative day if it were only a 24-hour period. Adam is assigned the task of naming the different kinds of animals. This is not a simple task of just picking a name randomly. In the ancient culture, names carried even more meaning than in our modern Western culture. Names were chosen to be descriptive, to reflect something about the person, animal, or thing. From the descriptive forms of the names Adam chose, it is obvious that it took some time, for the account literally reads "whatever the man called *every living creature*, that was its name."[72] (Genesis 2:19) For example, the Hebrew word for the "ass" refers to the usual reddened color. The Hebrew word for stork is the feminine form of the word meaning "loyal one."[73] This name is certainly a perfect fit, as the stork is known for the loving care it gives its young, and the loyalty of staying with its mate for life, something that would have been impossible to observe within a mere 24-hour day.

Regardless, it has been estimated, even if Adam has taken just one minute to name each pair, it would have taken 40 days with no sleep. It was only after Adam completed this task that Eve was created. Yet, even conceding the possibility that the process of naming the animals went quicker, because Adam named only the basic kinds of animals, like what went in Noah's ark at the time of the flood, which did not involve thousands of creatures, it would have taken weeks, possibly months, not a literal 24-hour day. It is during the process of Adam's naming the animals that it is discovered that "for the man no helper was found who was like him." (Genesis 2:20) Thus, we now see where the concern from Genesis 2:18 comes from, with God's reference to Adam's getting lonely. If it took weeks, months, or decades for Adam to complete his assignment of naming the animals, he would have had the time to grow lonely, but not in a couple hours as would be the case with a 24-hour day. Thus, the context here is that over a long period of time of naming the animals, Adam took note that he was alone while all the animals had mates. Let us take an extensive look at this again with the leading Hebrew language scholar of the 20th century, Dr. Gleason L. Archer.

It thus becomes clear in this present case, as we study the text of Genesis 1, that we must not short-circuit our responsibility of careful exegesis in order to ascertain as clearly

---

72. Walter A. Elwell and Barry J Beitzel, *Baker Encyclopedia of the Bible* (Grand Rapids, Mich.: Baker Book House, 1988), S. 93.

73. *Enhanced Brown-Driver-Briggs Hebrew and English Lexicon*. electronic ed. (Oak Harbor, WA : Logos Research Systems, 2000), S. 339.

as possible what the divine author meant by the language His inspired prophet (in this case probably Moses) was guided to employ. Is the true purpose of Genesis 1 to teach that all creation began just six twenty-four-hour days before Adam was "born"? Or is this just a mistaken inference that overlooks other biblical data having a direct bearing on this passage? To answer this question we must take careful note of what is said in Genesis 1:27 concerning the creation of man as the closing act of the sixth creative day. There it is stated that on that sixth day (apparently toward the end of the day, after all the animals had been fashioned and placed on the earth—therefore not long before sundown at the end of that same day), "God created man in His own image; He created them male and female." This can only mean that Eve was created in the closing hour of Day Six, along with Adam.

As we turn to Genesis 2, however, we find that a considerable interval of time must have intervened between the creation of Adam and the creation of Eve. In Gen. 2:15 we are told that Yahweh Elohim (i.e., the LORD God) put Adam in the garden of Eden as the idle environment for his development, and there he was to cultivate and keep the enormous park, with all its goodly trees, abundant fruit crop, and four mighty rivers that flowed from Eden to other regions of the Near East. In Gen 2:18 we read, "Then the LORD God said, 'It is not good for the man to be alone; I will make him a helper suitable for him.' " This statement clearly implies that Adam had been diligently occupied in his responsible task of pruning, harvesting fruit, and keeping the ground free of brush and undergrowth for a long enough period to lose his initial excitement and sense of thrill at this wonderful occupation in the beautiful paradise of Eden. He had begun to feel a certain lonesomeness and inward dissatisfaction.

In order to compensate for this lonesomeness, God then gave Adam a major assignment in natural history. He was to classify every species of animal and bird found in the preserve. With its five mighty rivers and broad expanse, the garden must have had hundreds of species of mammal, reptile, insect, and bird, to say nothing of the flying insects that also are indicated by the basic Hebrew term ʿôp̄ ("bird") (2:19). It took the Swedish scientist Linnaeus several decades to classify all the species known to European scientists in the eighteenth century.

Doubtless there were considerably more by that time than in Adam's day; and, of course, the range of fauna in Eden may have been more limited than those available to Linnaeus. But at the same time it must have taken a good deal of study for Adam to examine each specimen and decide on an appropriate name for it, especially in view of the fact that he had absolutely no human tradition behind him, so far as nomenclature was concerned. It must have required some years, or, at the very least, a considerable number of months for him to complete this comprehensive inventory of all the birds, beasts, and insects that populated the Garden of Eden.

Finally, after this assignment with all its absorbing interest had been completed, Adam felt a renewed sense of emptiness. Genesis 2:20 ends with the words "but for Adam no suitable helper was found." After this long and unsatisfying experience as a lonely bachelor, God saw that Adam was emotionally prepared for a wife—a "suitable helper." God, therefore, subjected him to a deep sleep, removed from his body the bone that was closest to his heart, and from that physical core of man fashioned the first woman. Finally God presented woman to Adam in all her fresh, unspoiled beauty, and Adam was ecstatic with joy.

As we have compared Scripture with Scripture (Gen. 1:27 with 2:15–22), it has become very apparent that Genesis 1 was never intended to teach that the sixth creative day, when Adam and Eve were both created, lasted a mere twenty-four hours. In view of the long interval of time between these two, it would seem to border on sheer irrationality to insist that all of Adam's experiences in Genesis 2:15–22 could have been crowded into the last hour or two of a literal twenty-four-hour day. The only reasonable conclusion to draw is that the purpose of Genesis 1 is not to tell how fast God performed His work of creation (though, of course, some of His acts, such as the creation of light on the first day, must have been instantaneous). Rather, its true purpose was to reveal that the Lord God who had revealed Himself to the Hebrew race and entered into personal covenant relationship with them was indeed the only true God, the Creator of all things that are. This stood in direct opposition to the religious notions of the heathen around them, who assumed the emergence of pantheon of gods in successive stages out of preexistent matter of unknown origin, actuated by forces for which there was no accounting.[74]

Below, we see more examples of accounts within creation that are not instantaneous. Those who favor literal 24-hour creation days really must ignore a lot of context that does not allow for a literal interpretation of the creation days.

Genesis 2:8-9 Updated American Standard Version (UASV)

8 And Jehovah God planted a garden toward the east, in Eden; and there he put the man whom he had formed. **9** And **out of the ground Jehovah God caused to grow every tree** that is pleasing to the sight and good for food; the tree of life also in the midst of the garden, and the tree of the knowledge of good and evil.

The straightforward reading of this text is that it is not an instantaneous creation. It is that Jehovah God planted the trees, and they grew as we understand trees grow, in a normal fashion.

Genesis 1:11-12 Updated American Standard Version (UASV)

11 And God said, "Let the earth sprout vegetation, plants yielding seed, and fruit trees bearing fruit in which is their seed, each according to its kind, on the earth." And it was so. **12** The earth **brought forth vegetation, plants yielding seed according to their own kinds**, and trees bearing fruit in which is their seed, each according to its kind. And God saw that it was good.

Here again, the straight-forward reading, we are seeing the natural process of all vegetation, as opposed to it being created instantly.

In addition, it should be noted that God's Word explicitly helps man to appreciate that a "day" to Jehovah God is not measured in the same way as man.

Psalm 90:4: For in Your sight a thousand years are like yesterday that passes by, like a few hours of the night.

2 Peter 3:8: Dear friends, don't let this one thing escape you: with the Lord one day is like 1,000 years, and 1,000 years like one day.

---

[74] Gleason L. Archer, New International Encyclopedia of Bible Difficulties, Zondervan's Understand the Bible Reference Series, 59-60 (Grand Rapids, MI: Zondervan Publishing House, 1982).

2 Peter 3:10: But the Day of the Lord will come like a thief; on that [day] the heavens will pass away with a loud noise, the elements will burn and be dissolved, and the earth and the works on it will be disclosed.

As we can see on the sixth creation day, we are introduced to the creation of both domestic and wild animals, these being in relation to what man could tame and use domestically, as opposed to what remain wild. Within this creation period was also the greatest of all creation, the creation of both man and woman. It with the creation of humans alone that it was said they were 'created in the image of God.'

Then there is the problem of the seventh day, as far as the young earth view is concerned: it never ended. There was no opening and closing, as occurred with the preceding six days; it is still in progress from the close of the sixth day, more than 6,000 years ago.

Hebrews 4:4, 5, 9–11: For somewhere He has spoken about the seventh day in this way: And on the seventh day God rested from all His works. Again, in that passage [He says], They will never enter My rest. A Sabbath rest remains, therefore, for God's people. For the person who has entered His rest has rested from his own works, just as God did from His. Let us then make every effort to enter that rest, so that no one will fall into the same pattern of disobedience.

Clearly, the context of God's Word as a whole shows the earth to be much older than 6,000+ years.

Habakkuk 3:6: He stood, and measured the earth; He beheld, and drove asunder the nations; And the *eternal mountains* were scattered; The *everlasting hills* did bow; His goings were as of old.

Micah 6:2: Hear, O ye mountains, Jehovah's controversy, and ye *enduring foundations of the earth*; for Jehovah hath a controversy with his people, and he will contend with Israel.

Proverbs 8:22, 23: Jehovah possessed me in the beginning of his way, Before his works of old. I was set up from everlasting, from the beginning, Before the earth was.

The writer of Proverbs is using the age of the earth to emphasize that wisdom is much older. But if one accepts the young-earth theory (4004 B.C.E. for the creation of man),[75] when Solomon, who died shortly after

---

75. Archbishop James Usher (1581–1656) developed a chronology of the Bible, and dated creation at 4004 B.C.E.

1000 B.C.E., wrote this, the earth would have been only about 3,000 years old—so not much of an emphasis.

Science has established that light travels at 186,282 miles per second. We know that it takes 100,000 years for light to cross our galaxy. We also know that it has taken hundreds of millions of years for the light of the stars we now see to reach the earth. Let us not repeat the Galileo history once more. It takes humility to learn from past experience. The Galileo conflict between science and the Church should at the very least help Christendom to avoid taking "day" as a literal 24-hour day when Scripture itself allows for another understanding; context weighs in that direction and science has established that the earth and the universe are far older than 6,000–10,000 years. Regardless of whether some scholars will concede to the correct understanding, this would in no way put the Bible in the wrong, for it is its interpreters who have misunderstood it. We must keep in mind that science (or the scientist) has no quarrel with the Bible: the quarrel would be with the misinterpretation of the teachers of Christendom, orthodox Jews, and others.

The website ChristianAnswers.Net concludes: "The lesson to be learned from Galileo, it appears, is not that the Church held too tightly to biblical truths; but rather that it did not hold tightly enough. It allowed Greek philosophy to influence its theology and held to tradition rather than to the teachings of the Bible. We must hold strongly to Biblical doctrine which has been achieved through sure methods of exegesis. We must never be satisfied with dogmas built upon philosophic traditions."[76] However, it is also true that science alone should not determine our interpretation, but it is to be used in a balanced way, as another source to consider.

The Copernican theory was, in fact, condemned by the theologians of the Inquisition and Pope Urban VIII. They argued that it contradicted the Bible: to be specific, Joshua's statement: "O sun, stand still . . . So the sun stood still, and the moon stopped." (Joshua 10:12, *ESV*) Of course, this is not meant to be taken literally. There are several reasonable explanations, one of which, I will give you here. Verse 13 says that "the sun stopped in the midst of heaven and did not hurry to set for about a whole day." This could simply allow for a slower movement of the earth, giving the appearance to an earthly observer that the sun and moon had stood still. As for another reasonable explanation, one Bible encyclopedia

76. http://www.christiananswers.net/q-eden/edn-c007.html. (Accessed January 28, 2010.)

comments: "While this could mean a stopping of earth's rotation, it could have been accomplished by other means, such as a refraction of solar and lunar light rays to produce the same effect." Therefore, once more, it becomes obvious that the Bible does not contradict itself.

Let us take another look at this again with the leading apologist scholar of the 20th century, Dr. Norman L. Geisler.

PROBLEM: The Bible says that God created the world in six days (Ex. 20:11). But modern science declares that it took billions of years. Both cannot be true.

SOLUTION: There are basically two ways to reconcile this difficulty. First, some scholars argue that modern science is wrong. They insist that the universe is only thousands of years old and that God created everything in six literal 24-hour days (= 144 hours). In favor of this view they offer the following:

1. The days of Genesis each have "evening and the morning," (cf. Gen. 1:5, 8, 13, 19, 23, 31), something unique to 24-hour days in the Bible.

2. The days were numbered (first, second, third, etc.), a feature found only with 24-hour days in the Bible.

3. Exodus 20: 11 compares the six days of creation with the six days of a literal work week of 144 hours.

4. There is scientific evidence to support a young age (of thousands of years) for the earth.

5. There is no way life could survive millions of years from day three (1:11) today four (1:14) without light.

Other Bible scholars claim that the universe could be billions of years old without sacrificing a literal understanding of Genesis 1 and 2. They argue that:

1. The days of Genesis 1 could have a time lapse before the days began (before Gen. 1:3), or a time gap between the days. There are gaps elsewhere in the Bible (cf. Matt. 1:8, where three generations are omitted, with 1 Chron. 3:11-14).

2. The same Hebrew word "day" (yam) is used in Genesis 1-2 as a period of time longer than 24 hours. For example, Genesis 2:4 uses it of the whole six day period of creation.

3. Sometimes the Bible uses the word "day" for long periods of time: "One day is as a thousand years" (2 Peter 3:8; cf. Ps. 90:4).

4. There are some indications in Genesis 1-2 that days could be longer than 24 hours:

a) On the third "day" trees grew from seeds to maturity and they bore like seeds (1:11-12). This process normally takes months or years.

b) On the sixth "day" Adam was created, went to sleep, named all the (thousands of) animals, looked for a helpmeet, went to sleep, and Eve was created from his rib. This looks like more than 24 hours' worth of activity.

c) The Bible says God "rested" on the seventh day (2:2), and that He is still in His rest from creation (Heb. 4:4). Thus, the seventh day is thousands of years long already. If so, then other days could be thousands of years too.

5. Exodus 20:11 could be making a unit-for-unit comparison between the days of Genesis and a work week (of 144 hours), not a minute-by-minute comparison.

Conclusion: There is no demonstrated contradiction of fact between Genesis 1 and science. There is only a conflict of interpretation. Either, most modern scientists are wrong in insisting the world is billions of years old, or else some Bible interpreters are wrong in insisting on only 144 hours of creation some several thousand years before Christ with no gaps allowing millions of years. But, in either case it is not a question of inspiration of Scripture, but of the interpretation of Scripture (and of the scientific data).[77]

In Summary

- The Hebrew word for day that was used for the creation days of Genesis chapter 1 is the same word used at Genesis 2:4 as a reference to the whole of the creative period, six days, "in the day that . . ."

---

[77] Thomas Howe; Norman L. Geisler. *The Big Book of Bible Difficulties: Clear and Concise Answers from Genesis to Revelation* (Kindle Locations 356-375). Kindle Edition.

- The Bible uses the word for "day" as longer periods than a 24-hour day "one day is as a thousand years." (2 Peter 3:8; Psalm 90:4)

- There are indicators within the first two chapters that we are dealing with periods longer than 24-hour days.

(1) **Third Day**: At Genesis 1:11-12, we find that trees grew from seeds to maturity, and produced seeds of their kind. This takes months, even years.

(2) **Sixth day**: We find Adam was created, went to sleep, named thousands of animals (names that indicate observation of the animals), grew lonely (looking for a helper), went to sleep, Eve was produced out of Adam's rib. This is obviously longer than 24 hours.

(3) **Seventh Day**: Genesis 2:2 informs us that God "proceeded to rest."[78] The reader will note that Hebrews 4:4 shows that God is still in his rest from the ending of the six creative days. Therefore, the seventy day has been running for thousands if years thus far, which allows the other creative days to be thousands of years long.

As it usually turns out, the so-called contradiction between science and God's Word lies at the feet of those who are interpreting Scripture incorrectly. To repeat the sentiments of Galileo when writing to a pupil— Galileo expressed the same sentiments: "Even though Scripture cannot err, its interpreters and expositors can, in various ways. One of these, very serious and very frequent, would be when they always want to stop at the purely literal sense."[79] I believe that today's scholars, in hindsight, would have no problem agreeing.

---

[78] Why do I have it rendered as a continuous, "proceeded to rest", when most translations read "he rested"? Heb., waiyishboth (imperfect sequential): The verb is in the imperfect state denoting incomplete or continuous action, or action in progress.

79. Letter from Galileo to Benedetto Castelli, December 21, 1613.

Review Questions

- From whose standpoint are the Genesis events described? How does the description of the luminaries indicate this?

- What indication is there in the creation account itself that the word "day" does not mean just a 24-hour period?

- What is one meaning of the Hebrew word for "day" that indicates longer periods can be understood?

- Why does the use of "evening" and "morning" not necessarily limit a "day" to 24 hours?

- What other uses show "day" could be more than 24 hours?

APPENDIX B Bible Difficulties Explained

IT SEEMS THAT the charge that the Bible contradicts itself has been made more and more in the last 20 years. Generally, those making such claims are merely repeating what they have heard, because most have not even read the Bible, let alone done an in-depth study of it. I do not wish, however, to set aside all concerns as though they have no merit. There are many who raise legitimate questions that seem, on the surface anyway, to be about well-founded contradiction. Sadly, these issues have caused many to lose their faith in God's Word, the Bible. The purpose of this books is, to help its readers to be able to defend the Bible against Bible critics (1 Pet. 3:15), to contend for the faith (Jude 1:3), and help those, who have begun to doubt. – Jude 1:22-23.

Before we begin explaining things, let us jump right in, getting our feet wet, and deal with two major Bible difficulties, so we can see that there are reasonable, logical answers. After that, we will delve deeper into explaining Bible difficulties.

Is God permitting Human Sacrifice at Judges 11:30-31?

Judges 11:29-34, 37-41 English Standard Version (ESV)

29 Then the Spirit of the Lord was upon Jephthah, and he passed through Gilead and Manasseh and passed on to Mizpah of Gilead, and from Mizpah of Gilead he passed on to the Ammonites. **30** And Jephthah **made a vow** to the Lord and said, "If you will give the Ammonites into my hand, **31** then **whatever**[80] comes out from the doors of my house to meet me when I return in peace from the Ammonites shall be the Lord's, and I will offer it up for a burnt offering." **32** So Jephthah crossed over to the Ammonites to fight against them, and the Lord gave them into his hand. **33** And he struck them from Aroer to the neighborhood of Minnith, twenty cities, and as far as Abel-keramim, with a great blow. So the Ammonites were subdued before the people of Israel.

---

[80] Whoever

34 Then Jephthah came to his home at Mizpah. And behold, **his daughter came out** to meet him with tambourines and with dances. She was his only child; besides her he had neither son nor daughter.

37 So she said to her father, "Let this thing be done for me: leave me alone two months, that I may go up and down on the mountains and weep for my virginity, I and my companions." **38** So he said, "Go." Then he sent her away for two months, and she departed, **she and her companions, and wept for her virginity** on the mountains. **39** And at the end of two months, she returned to her father, who **did with her according to his vow that he had made**. She had never known a man [been intimate with a man], and it became a custom in Israel **40** that the daughters of Israel went year by year to **lament [or commemorate] the daughter** of Jephthah the Gileadite four days in the year.

It is true; to infer that having the idea of an animal sacrifice would really have not been an impressive vow, which the context requires. Human sacrifice would be repugnant, if we are talking about taking a life. Jephthah had no sons, so he likely knew it was the daughter, who would come to greet him.

First, the text does not say he killed his daughter. The idea of some that he did kill her is concluded only by an inference. While it is not good policy to interpret backward, using Paul on Judges, he does say humans are to be "**as a living sacrifice.**" Therefore, Jephthah could have offered his daughter at the temple, "as a living sacrifice" in service, like Samuel.

This is not to be taken dismissively, because under Jewish backgrounds, it is no small thing to offer a **perpetual virginity** as a sacrifice. This would mean Jephthah's lineage would not be carried on, the family name, was no more.

Second, the context says she went out to weep for two months, not mourn her death. It says, "she left with her friends and **mourned her virginity**."

If she was facing impending death, she could have married, and spent that last two months as a married woman. There would be absolutely no reason for her to mourn her virginity, if she were not facing perpetual virginity. – Exodus 38:8; 1 Samuel 2:22

Third, it was completely forbidden to offer a human sacrifice. – Leviticus 18:21; 20:2-5; Deuteronomy 12:31; 18:10

Imagine an Israelite believing that he could please God with a human sacrifice that was intended to offer up a human life. To do so would have been a rejection of Jehovah's Sovereignty (the very person you are asking for help), and a rejection of the Law that made them a special people. Worse still, this interpretation would have us believe that Jehovah knew this was coming, allowed the vow, and then aided this type of man to succeed over his enemies.

The last point is simple enough. If such a man as one who would make such a vow, in gross violation of the law, and then carry it out; there is no way he would be mentioned by Paul in Hebrews chapter 11.

There is no way God would have granted and helped in Jephthah's initial success knowing the vow that was coming, because both Jehovah and Jephthah would be as bad as the Canaanites. There is no way that God would accept such a vow and then go on to help Jephthah with his enemies yet again. Then, to allow such a vow to be carried out, to then put Jephthah on the wall of star witnesses for God in Hebrews chapter 11.

Does Isaiah 45:7 mean that God Is the Author of Evil?

Isaiah 45:7 King James Version (KJV)

7 I form the light, and create darkness: I make peace, and **create evil**: I the Lord do all these things.

Isaiah 45:7 English Standard Version (ESV)

7 I form light and create darkness,

   I make well-being and **create calamity**,

   I am the Lord, who does all these things.[81]

Encarta Dictionary: (Evil) (1) morally bad: profoundly immoral or wrong (2) deliberately causing great harm, pain, or upset

QUESTION: Is this view of evil always the case? No, as you will see below.

Some apologetic authors try to say, 'we are not understanding Isaiah 45:7 correctly, because there are other verses that say God is not evil (1 John 1:5), cannot look approvingly on evil (Hab. 1:13), and cannot be tempted by evil. (Jam. 1:13)' Well, while all of these things are Scripturally true, the question at hand is not: Is God evil, can God approvingly look on evil, or can God be tempted with evil? Those questions are not relevant to the one at hand, as God cannot be those things, and at the

---

[81] See Jeremiah 18:11, Lamentations 3:18, and Amos 3:6

same time, he can be the yes to our question. The question is, is God the author, the creator of evil?

We would hardly argue that God was **not just** in his bringing "calamity" or "evil" down on Adam and Eve. Thus, we have Isaiah 45:7 saying that God is the creator of "calamity" or "evil."

Let us begin simple, without trying to be philosophical. When God removed Adam and Eve from the Garden of Eden, he sentenced them and humanity to sickness, old age, and death. (Rom. 5:8; i.e., enforce penalty for sin), which was to bring "calamity" or "evil" upon humankind. Therefore, as we can "evil" does not always mean wrongdoing. Other examples of God bringing "calamity" or "evil" are Noah and the flood, the Ten Plagues of Egypt, and the destruction of the Canaanites. These acts of evil were not acts of wrongdoing. Rather, they were righteous and just, because God, the Creator of all things, was administering justice to wrongdoers, to sinners. He warned the perfect first couple what the penalty was for sin. He warned the people for a hundred years by Noah's preaching. He warned the Canaanites centuries before.

Nevertheless, there are times, when God extends mercy, refraining from the execution of his righteous judgment to one worthy of calamity. For example, he warned Nineveh, the city of blood, and they repented, so he pardoned them. (Jon 3:10) God has made it a practice to warn persons of the results of sin, giving them undeservedly many opportunities to change their ways. – Ezekiel 33:11.

God cannot sin; it is impossible for him to do so. So, when did he create evil? Without getting into the eternity of his knowing what he was going to do, and when, let us just say, evil did not exist when he was the only person in existence. We might say the idea of evil existed because he knew what he was going to do. However, the moment he created creatures (spirit and human), the potential for evil came into existence because both have a free will to sin. Evil became a reality the moment Satan entertained the idea of causing Adam to sin, to get humanity for himself, and then acted on it.

God has the right and is just to bring calamity of or evil down on anyone that is an unrepentant sinner. God did not even have to give us the underserved kindness of offering us his Son. God is the author or agent of evil regardless of the source books that claim otherwise. If he had never created free will beings, evil would have never gone from the idea of evil to the potential of evil, to the existence of evil. However, God felt that it was better to get the sinful state out of angel and human existence, recover, and then any who would sin thereafter, he would be justified in handing out evil or calamity to just that person or angel alone.

Who among us would argue that he should have created humans and angels like robots, automatons with no free will? The moment he chose the free will, he moved evil from an idea to a potential, and Satan moved it to a reality. God has a moral nature that does not bring about evil and sin when he is the only person in existence. However, the moment he created beings in his image, who had the potential to sin, he brought about evil. The moment we have a moral code of good and evil that is placed upon one's with free will; then, we have evil.

In English, the very comprehensive Hebrew word ra' is variously translated as "bad," "downcast (sad, NASB)," "ugly," "evil," "grievous (distressing, NASB)," "sore," "selfish (stingy, HCSB)," and "envious," depending upon the context. (Gen 2:9; 40:7; 41:3; Ex 33:4; Deut. 6:22; 28:35; Pro 23:6; 28:22)

Evil as an adjective **describes** the **quality of** a class of people, places, or things, or of a specific person, place, or thing

Evil as a noun, **defines** the **nature** of a class of people, places, or things, or of a specific person, place, or thing (e.g., the evil one, evil eye)**.**

We can agree that "evil" is a thing. Create means to bring something into existence, be it people, places, or things, as well something abstract, for lack of a better word at the moment. We would agree that when God was alone evil was not a reality, it did not exist? We would agree that the moment that God created free will creatures (angels and humans), creating humans in his image, with his moral nature, he also brought the potential for evil into existence, and it was realized by Satan?

Inerrancy: Can the Bible Be trusted?

If the Bible is the Word of God, it should be in complete agreement throughout; there should be no contradictions. Yet, the rational mind must ask, why is it that some passages appear to be contradictions when compared with others? For example, Numbers 25:9 tells us that 24,000 died from the scourge, whereas at 1 Corinthians 10:8, the apostle Paul says it was 23,000. This would seem to be a clear error. Before addressing such matters, let us first look at some background information.

Full inerrancy in this book means that the original writings are fully without error in all that they state, as are the words. The words were not dictated (automaton), but the intended meaning is inspired, as are the words that convey that meaning. The Author allowed the writer to use his style of writing, yet controlled the meaning to the extent of not allowing the writer to choose a wrong word, which would not convey the intended meaning. Other more liberal-minded persons hold with *partial inerrancy*, which claims that as far as faith is concerned, this portion of God's Word is without error, but that there are historical, geographical, and scientific errors.

There are several different levels of inerrancy. *Absolute Inerrancy* is the belief that the Bible is fully true and exact in every way; including not only relationships and doctrine, but also science and history. In other words, all information is completely exact. *Full Inerrancy* is the belief that the Bible was not written as a science or historical textbook, but is phenomenological, in that it is written from the human perspective. In other words, speaking of such things as the sun rising, the four corners of the earth, or the rounding off of number approximations are all from a human perspective. *Limited Inerrancy* is the belief that the Bible is meant only as a reflection of God's purposes and will, so the science and history is the understanding of the author's day, and is limited. Thus, the Bible is susceptible to errors in these areas. *Inerrancy of Purpose* is the belief that it is only inerrant in the purpose of bringing its readers to a saving faith. The Bible is not about facts, but about persons and relationships, thus, it is subject to error. *Inspired: Not Inerrant* is the belief that its authors are human and thus subject to human error. It should be noted that this author holds the position of full inerrancy.

For many today, the Bible is nothing more than a book written by men. The Bible critic believes the Bible to be full of myths and legends, contradictions, and geographical, historical, and scientific errors. University professor Gerald A. Larue had this to say, "The views of the writers as expressed in the Bible reflect the ideas, beliefs, and concepts current in their own times and are limited by the extent of knowledge in those times."[82] On the other hand, the Bible's authors claim that their writings were inspired of God, as Holy Spirit moved them along. We will discover shortly that the Bible critics have much to say, but it is inflated or empty. Moreover, as has been said many times throughout this book, the Bible critic has been repeating the same charges for over 150-years, even though we have long had answers to those questions.

2 Timothy 3:16-17 Updated American Standard Version (UASV)

---

[82] Gerald Larue, "The Bible as a Political Weapon," *Free Inquiry* (Summer 1983): 39.

16 All Scripture is inspired by God and profitable for teaching, for reproof, for correction, for training in righteousness; **17** so that the man of God may be fully competent, equipped for every good work.

2 Peter 1:21 Updated American Standard Version (UASV)

21 for no prophecy was ever produced by the will of man, but men carried along by the Holy Spirit spoke from God.

The question remains as to whether the Bible is a book written by imperfect men and full of errors, or is written by imperfect men, but inspired of God. If the Bible is just another book by imperfect man, there is no hope for humankind. If it is inspired of God and without error, although penned by imperfect men, we have the hope of everything that it offers: a rich happy life now by applying counsel that lies within and the real life that is to come, everlasting life. This author contends that the Bible is inspired of God and free of human error, although written by imperfect humans.

Before we take on the critics who seem to sift the Scriptures looking for problematic verses, let us take a moment to reflect on how we should approach these alleged problem texts. The critic's argument goes something like this: 'If God does not err and the Bible is the Word of God, then the Bible should not have one single error or contradiction, yet it is full of errors and contradictions.' If the Bible is riddled with nothing but contradictions and errors as the critics would have us believe, why, out of 31,173 verses in the Bible, should there be only 2-3 thousand Bible difficulties that are called into question, this being less than ten percent of the whole?

First, let it be said that it is every Christian's obligation to get a deeper understanding of God's Word, just as the apostle Paul told Timothy,

1 Timothy 4:15-16 Updated American Standard Version (UASV)

15 Practice these things, be absorbed in them, so that your progress will be evident to all. **16** Pay close attention to yourself and to your teaching; persevere in these things, for as you do this you will ensure salvation both for yourself and for those who hear you.[83]

---

[83] **4:15 progress**. The word was used in military terms of an advancing force and in general terms of advancement in learning, understanding, or knowledge. Paul exhorted Timothy to let his progress toward Christlikeness be evident to all. **4:16 to yourself and to the doctrine**. The priorities of a godly leader are summed up in his personal holiness and

Paul also told the Corinthians:

2 Corinthians 10:4-5 Updated American Standard Version (UASV)

4 For the weapons of our warfare are not of the flesh[84] but powerful to God for destroying strongholds.[85] **5** We are destroying speculations and every lofty thing raised up against the knowledge of God, and we are taking every thought captive to the obedience of Christ,

Paul also told the Philippians:

Philippians 1:7 Updated American Standard Version (UASV)

7 It is right for me to feel thus about you all, because I hold you in my heart, for you are all partakers with me of grace, both in my imprisonment and in the defense and confirmation of the gospel.

In being able to defend against the modern-day critic, one has to be able to reason from the Scriptures and overturn the critic's argument(s) with mildness. If someone were to approach us about an alleged error or contradiction, what should we do? We should be frank and honest. If we do not have an answer, we should admit such. If the text in question gives the appearance of difficulty, we should admit this as well. If we are unsure as to how we should answer, we can simply say that we will look into it and get back with them, returning with a reasonable answer.

However, do not express disbelief and doubt to your critics, because they will be emboldened in their disbelief. It will put them on the offense and you on the defense. With great confidence, you can express that there is an answer. The Bible has withstood the test of 2,000 years of persecution and is the most printed book of all time, currently being translated into 2,287 languages. If these critical questions were so threatening, the Bible would not be the book that it is.

---

public teaching. All of Paul's exhortations in verses 6–16 fit into one or the other of those two categories. **you will save . . . yourself**. Perseverance in believing the truth always accompanies genuine conversion (see note on Matt. 24:13; cf. John 8:31; Rom. 2:7; Phil. 2:12, 13; Col. 1:23). **those who hear you**. By careful attention to his own godly life and faithful preaching of the Word, Timothy would continue to be the human instrument God used to bring the gospel and to save some who heard him. Though salvation is God's work, it is His pleasure to do it through human instruments.–MacArthur, John (2005-05-09). *The MacArthur Bible Commentary* (Kindle Locations 60174-60182). Thomas Nelson. Kindle Edition.

[84] That is *merely human*

[85] That is *tearing down false arguments*

When you are pursuing the text in question, be unwavering in purpose, or resolved to find an answer. In some cases, it may take hours of digging to find the solution. Consider this: as you resolve these difficulties, you are also building your faith that God's Word is inerrant. Moreover, you will want to do preventative maintenance in your personal study. As you are doing your Bible reading, take note of these surface discrepancies and resolve them as you work your way through the Bible. Make this a part of your prayers as well. I recommend the following program. At the end of this chapter I list several books that deal with difficult passages. As you read your Bible from Genesis to Revelation, do not attempt it in one year; make it a four-year program. Use a good exegetical commentary like *The New International Commentary of the Old and New Testament* (NICOT/NICNT) or *The New American Commentary* set, and *The Big Book of Bible Difficulties* by Norman L. Geisler, as well as *The Encyclopedia of Bible Difficulties* by Gleason Archer.

You should be aware that the originally written books were penned by men under inspiration. In fact, we do not have those originals, what textual scholars call autographs, but we do have thousands of copies. The copyists, however, were not inspired; therefore, as one might expect, throughout the first 1,400 years of copying, thousands of errors were transmitted into the texts that were being copied by imperfect hands that were not under inspiration when copying. Yet, the next 450 years saw a restoration of the text by textual scholars from around the world. Therefore, while many of our best literal translations today may not be inspired, they are a mirror-like reflection of the autographs by way of textual criticism.[86] Therefore, the fallacy could be with the copyist error that has simply not been weeded out. In addition, you must keep in mind that God's Word is without error, but our interpretation and understanding of that Word is not.

In this chapter, we are not going to take the space that we will in later chapters that are dedicated to one difficulty. Here, in short, we will address a number of them. Before looking at a few examples, it should be noted that the Bible is made up of 66 smaller books that were hand-written over a period of 1,600 years, having some 40 writers of various trades such as shepherd, king, priest, tax collector, governor, physician, copyist, fisherman, and tentmaker. Therefore, it should not surprise us that some difficulties are encountered as we casually read through the

---

[86] Textual criticism is the study of copies of any written work of which the autograph (original) is unknown, with the purpose of ascertaining the original text. Harold J. Green, Introduction to New Testament Textual Criticism (Peabody, MA: Hendrickson, 1995), 1.

Bible. Yet, if one were to take a deeper look, one would find that these difficulties are easily explained. Let us take a few pages to examine some passages that have been under attack.

Again, our objective here is not to be exhaustive, not even close. What we are looking to do is cover a few alleged contradictions and a couple of alleged mistakes. This is to give you, the reader, a small sampling of the reasonable answers that you will find in the recommended books at the end of the chapter. Remember, your Bible is a sword that you must use both offensively and defensively. One must wonder how long a warrior of ancient times would last who was not expertly trained in the use of his weapon. Let us look at a few scriptures that support our need to learn our Bible well so will be able to defend what we believe to be true.

When "false apostles, deceitful workmen, disguising themselves as apostles of Christ" were causing trouble in the congregation in Corinth, the apostle Paul wrote that under such circumstances, we are to *tear down their arguments* and *take every thought captive*. (2 Corinthians 10:4, 5; 11:13–15) All who present critical arguments against God's Word, or contrary to it, can have their arguments overturned by the Christian who is able and ready to defend that Word in mildness. – 2 Timothy 2:24–26.

1 Peter 3:15 Updated American Standard Version (UASV)

[87] but sanctify Christ as Lord in your hearts, always being prepared to make a defense[87] to anyone who asks you for a reason for the hope that is in you; yet do it with gentleness and respect;

Peter says that we need to be prepared to make a *defense*. The Greek word behind the English 'defense' is *apologia*, which is actually a legal term that refers to the defense of a defendant in court. Our English apologetics is just what Peter spoke of, having the ability to give a reason to any who may challenge us, or to answer those who are not challenging us but who have honest questions that deserve to be answered.

2 Timothy 2:24-25 Updated American Standard Version (UASV)

[24] For a slave of the Lord does not need to fight, but needs to be kind to all, qualified to teach, showing restraint when wronged [25] with

---

[87] Or *argument*; or *explanation*

gentleness correcting those who are in opposition, if perhaps God may grant them repentance leading to accurate knowledge[88] of the truth,

Look at the Greek word (*epignosis*) behind the English "knowledge" in the above. "It is more intensive than *gnosis* (1108), knowledge, because it expresses a more thorough participation in the acquiring of knowledge on the part of the learner."[89] The requirement of all of the Lord's servants is that they be able to teach, but not in a quarrelsome way, and in a way to correct his opponents with mildness. Why? Because the purpose of it all is that by God, and through the Christian teacher, one may come to repentance and begin taking in an accurate knowledge of the truth.

Inerrancy: Practical Principles to Overcoming Bible Difficulties

Below are several ways of looking at the Bible that enable the reader to see he is not dealing with an error or a contradiction, but rather a Bible difficulty.

Different Points of View

At times, you may have two different writers who are writing from two different points of view.

Numbers 35:14 New International Version (NIV)

¹⁴ Give three on this side of the Jordan and three in Canaan as cities of refuge.

Joshua 22:4 New International Version (NIV)

⁴ Now that the Lord your God has given them rest as he promised, return to your homes in the land that Moses the servant of the Lord gave you on the other side of the Jordan.

Here we see that Moses is speaking about the east side of the Jordan when he says "on this side of the Jordan." Joshua, on the other hand, is also speaking about the east side of the Jordan when he says "on the other side of the Jordan." So, who is correct? Both are. When Moses was

---

[88] *Epignosis* is a strengthened or intensified form of *gnosis* (*epi*, meaning "additional"), meaning, "true," "real," "full," "complete" or "accurate," depending upon the context. Paul and Peter alone use *epignosis*.

[89] Spiros Zodhiates, *The Complete Word Study Dictionary: New Testament*, Electronic ed. (Chattanooga, TN: AMG Publishers, 2000, c1992, c1993), S. G1922.

penning Numbers the Israelites had not yet crossed the Jordan River, so the east side was "this side," the side he was on. On the other hand, when Joshua penned his book, the Israelites had crossed the Jordan, so the east side was just as he had said, "on the other side of the Jordan." Thus, we should not assume that two different writers are writing from the same perspective.

A Careful Reading

At times, it may simply be a case of needing to slow down and carefully read the account, considering exactly what is being said. Many times, we are reading the Bible as if we are reading a novel, which will hamper any serious growth in knowledge and understanding.

Joshua 18:28 New American Standard Bible (NASB)

[28] and Zelah, Haeleph and the Jebusite (that is, Jerusalem), Gibeah, Kiriath; fourteen cities with their villages. This is the inheritance of the sons of Benjamin according to their families.

Judges 1:21 New International Version (NIV)

[21] The Benjamites, however, did not drive out the Jebusites, who were living in Jerusalem; to this day the Jebusites live there with the Benjamites.

Joshua 15:63 New International Version (NIV)

[63] Judah could not dislodge the Jebusites, who were living in Jerusalem; to this day the Jebusites live there with the people of Judah.

Judges 1:8-9 New American Standard Bible (NASB)

[8] Then the sons of Judah fought against Jerusalem and captured it and struck it with the edge of the sword and set the city on fire. [9] Afterward the sons of Judah went down to fight against the Canaanites living in the hill country and in the Negev and in the lowland.

2 Samuel 5:5-9 New American Standard Bible (NASB)

[5] At Hebron he reigned over Judah seven years and six months, and in Jerusalem he reigned thirty-three years over all Israel and Judah.

[6] Now the king and his men went to Jerusalem against the Jebusites, the inhabitants of the land, and they said to David, "You shall not come in here, but the blind and lame will turn you away"; thinking, "David cannot enter here." [7] Nevertheless, David captured the stronghold of

Zion, that is the city of David. **8** David said on that day, "Whoever would strike the Jebusites, let him reach the lame and the blind, who are hated by David's soul, through the water tunnel." Therefore they say, "The blind or the lame shall not come into the house." **9** So David lived in the stronghold and called it the city of David. And David built all around from the Millo and inward.

There is no doubt that even the advanced Bible reader of many years can come away confused because the above accounts seem to be contradictory. In Joshua 18:28 and Judges 1:21, we see that Jerusalem was an inheritance of the tribe of Benjamin, yet the Benjamites were unable to conquer Jerusalem. But in Joshua 15:63 we see that the tribe of Judah could not conquer them either, with the reading giving the impression that it was a part of their inheritance. In Judges 1:8, however, Judah was eventually able to conquer Jerusalem and burn it with fire. Yet, to add even more to the confusion, we find at 2 Samuel 5:5–8 that David is said to have conquered Jerusalem hundreds of years later.

Now that we have the particulars, let us look at it more clearly. The boundary between Benjamin's inheritances ran right through the middle of Jerusalem. Joshua 8:28 is correct, in that what would later be called the "city of David" was in the territory of Benjamin, but it also in part crossed over the line into the territory of Judah, causing both tribes to go to war against this Jebusite city. It is also true that the tribe of Benjamin was unable to conquer the city and that the tribe of Judah eventually did. However, if you look at Judges 1:9 again, you will see that Judah did not finish the job entirely and moved on to conquer other areas. This allowed the remaining ones to regroup and form a resistance that neither Benjamin nor Judah could overcome, so these Jebusites remained until the time of David, hundreds of years later.

Intended Meaning of Writer

First, the Bible student needs to understand the level that the Bible intends to be exact in what is written. If Jim told a friend that 650 graduated with him from high school in 1984, it is not challenged, because it is all too clear that he is using rounded numbers and is not meaning to be exactly precise. This is how God's Word operates as well. Sometimes it means to be exact, at other times, it is simply rounding numbers, in other cases, the intention of the writer is a general reference, to give readers of that time and succeeding generations some perspective. Did Samuel, the author of judges, intend to pen a book on the chronology of Judges, or was his focus on the falling away, oppression, and the rescue by a judge, repeatedly. Now, it would seem that Jeremiah, the author of 1 Kings was more interested in giving his readers an exact number of years.

Acts 2:41 English Standard Version (ESV)

41 So those who received his word were baptized, and there were added that day about three thousand souls.

As you can see here, numbers within the Bible are often used with approximations. This is a frequent practice even today, in both written works and verbal conversation. It cannot be repeated enough, it is what the author meant by the words that he used.

Acts 7:2-3 English Standard Version (ESV)

2 And Stephen said:

"Brothers and fathers, hear me. The God of glory appeared to our father Abraham when he was in Mesopotamia, before he lived in Haran, **3** and said to him, 'Go out from your land and from your kindred and go into the land that I will show you.'

If you were to check the Hebrew Scriptures at Genesis 12:1, you would find that what is claimed to have been said by God to Abraham is not quoted word-for-word; it is simply a paraphrase. This is a normal practice within Scripture and in writing in general.

Numbers 34:15 English Standard Version (ESV)

15 The two tribes and the half-tribe have received their inheritance beyond the Jordan east of Jericho, toward the sunrise."

Just as you would read in today's local newspaper, the Bible writer has written from the human standpoint, how it appeared to him. The Bible also speaks of "to the end of the earth" (Psalm 46:9), "from the four corners of the earth" (Isa 11:12), and "the four winds of the earth" (Revelation 7:1). These phrases are still used today. Again, it is what the author meant by the words that he used as would have been understood by his readers.

Unexplained Does Not Mean Unexplainable

Considering that there are 31,173 verses in the Bible, encompassing 66 books written by about 40 writers, ranging from shepherds, to kings, an army general, fishermen, tax collector, a physician and on and on, and being penned over a 1,600 year period, one does find a few hundred

Bible difficulties (about one percent). However, 99 percent of those are explainable. Yet no one wants to be so arrogant to say that he can explain them all. It has nothing to do with the inadequacy of God's Word, but is based on human understanding. In many cases, science or archaeology and the field of custom and culture of ancient peoples has helped explain difficulties in hundreds of passages. Therefore, there may be less than one percent left to be answered, yet our knowledge of God's Word continues to grow. Again, the Bible critic is entirely dependent on the Christian's failing to buy out the times to investigate these challenges. So much so that the critic makes the same arguments over and over with each Christian, knowing there has been an answer for over 150-years.

Guilty Until Proven Innocent

This is exactly the perception that the critic has of God's Word. The legal principle of being "innocent until proven guilty" afforded mankind in courts of justice is withheld from the very Word of God. What is ironic here is that this policy has contributed to these Bible critics looking foolish over and over again when something comes to light that vindicates the portion of Scripture they are challenging.

Daniel 5:1 English Standard Version (ESV)

[1] King Belshazzar made a great feast for a thousand of his lords and drank wine in front of the thousand.

Bible critics had long claimed that Belshazzar was not known outside of the book Daniel; therefore, they argue that Daniel was mistaken. Yet it hardly seems prudent to argue error from absence of outside evidence. Just because archaeology had not discovered such a person did not mean that Daniel was wrong, or that such a person did not exist. In 1854, some small clay cylinders were discovered in modern-day southern Iraq, which would have been the city of Ur in ancient Babylonia. The cuneiform documents were a prayer of King Nabonidus for "Bel-sar-ussur, my eldest son." These tablets also showed that this "Bel-sar-ussur" had secretaries as well as a household staff. Other tablets were discovered a short time later that showed that the kingship was entrusted to this eldest son as a coregent while his father was away.

He entrusted the 'Camp' to his oldest (son), the firstborn [Belshazzar], and the troops everywhere in the country he ordered under his (command). He let (everything) go, entrusted the kingship to him and, himself, he [Nabonidus] started out for a long journey, the (military) forces of Akkad marching with him; he turned towards Tema (deep) in the west."[90]

Ignoring Literary Styles

The Bible is a diverse book when it comes to literary styles: narrative, poetic, prophetic, and apocalyptic; also containing parables, metaphors, similes, hyperbole, and other figures of speech. Too often, these alleged errors are the result of a reader taking a figure of speech as literal, or reading a parable as though it is a narrative. Poetry, parables, prophecy and the like have a license to exaggerate or use figurative language. Once we know what the author meant by his exaggerated language, this is what we take literally.

Matthew 24:35 English Standard Version (ESV)

[35] Heaven and earth will pass away, but my words will not pass away.

If some do not recognize that they are dealing with a figure of speech, they are bound to come away with the wrong meaning. Some have concluded from Matthew 24:35 that Jesus was speaking of an eventual destruction of the earth. This is hardly the case, as his listeners would not have understood it that way based on their understanding of the Old Testament. They would have understood that he was simply being emphatic about the words he spoke, using hyperbole. What he was conveying is that his words are more enduring than heaven and earth, and with heaven and earth being understood as eternal, this merely conveyed even more so that Jesus' words could be trusted.

Two Accounts of the Same Incident

If you were to speak to officers that take accident reports for their police department, you would find that there is cohesion in the accounts, but each person has merely witnessed aspects that have stood out to them. We will see that this is the case as well with the examples below, which is the same account in two different gospels:

Matthew 8:5 English Standard Version (ESV)

[5] When he had entered Capernaum, a centurion came forward to him, appealing to him,

---

[90] J. Pritchard, ed., *Ancient Near Eastern Texts* (1974), 313.

Luke 7:3 English Standard Version (ESV)

³ When the centurion heard about Jesus, he sent to him elders of the Jews, asking him to come and heal his servant.

Immediately we see the problem of whether the centurion or the elders of the Jews spoke with Jesus. The solution is not really hidden from us. Which of the two accounts is the more detailed account? You are correct if you said Luke. The centurion sent the elders of the Jews to represent him to Jesus, so; that whatever response Jesus might give, it would be as though he were addressing the centurion; therefore, Matthew gave his readers the basic thought, not seeing the need of mentioning the elders of the Jews aspect. This is how a representative was viewed in the first century, just as some countries see ambassadors today as being the very person they represent. Therefore, both Matthew and Luke are correct.

Man's Fallible Interpretations

Inspiration by God is infallible, without error. Imperfect man and his interpretations over the centuries, as bad as many of them have been, should not cast a shadow over God's inspired Word. The entire Word of God has one meaning and one meaning only for every penned word, which is what God willed to be conveyed by the human writer he chose to use.

The Autograph Alone Is Inspired and Inerrant

It has been argued by conservative scholars that only the autograph manuscripts were inspired and inerrant, not the copying of those manuscripts over the next 3,000 years for the Old Testament and 1,500 years for the New Testament. While I would agree with this position as well, it should be noted that we do not possess the autographs, so to argue that they are inerrant is to speak of nonexistent documents. However, it should be further understood that through the science of textual criticism, we can establish a mirror reflection of the autograph manuscripts. B. F. Westcott, F. J. A. Hort, F. F. Bruce, and many other textual scholars would agree with Norman L Geisler's assessment: "The New Testament, then, has not only survived in more manuscripts than any other book from antiquity, but it has survived in a purer form than any other great book—*a form that is 99.5 percent pure.*"[91]

An example of a copyist error can be found in Luke's genealogy of Jesus at Luke 3:35–37. In verse 37 you will find a Cainan, and in verse 36 you will find a second Cainan between Arphaxad (Arpachshad) and Shelah. As one can see from most footnotes in different study Bibles, the Cainan in verse 36 is seen as a scribal error, and is not found in the Hebrew Old Testament, the Samaritan Pentateuch, or the Aramaic Targums, but is found in the Greek Septuagint. (Genesis 10:24; 11:12, 13; 1 Chronicles 1:18, but not 1 Chronicles 1:24) It seems quite unlikely that it was in the earlier copies of the Septuagint, because the first-century Jewish historian Josephus lists Shelah next as the son of Arphaxad, and Josephus normally followed the Septuagint.[92] So one might ask why this second Cainan is found in the translations at all if this is the case? The manuscripts that do contain this second Cainan are some of the best manuscripts that are used in establishing the original text: 01 B L A¹ 33 (Kainam); A 038 044 0102 A¹³ (Kainan).

Look at the Context

Many alleged inconsistencies disappear by simply looking at the context. Taking words out of context can distort their meaning. *Merriam-Webster's Collegiate Dictionary* defines context as **"the parts of a discourse that surround a word or passage and can throw light on its meaning."**[93] Context can also be "the circumstances or events that form the environment within which something exists or takes place." If we were to look in a thesaurus for a synonym, we would find "background" for this second meaning. At 2 Timothy 2:15, the apostle Paul brings home the point of why context is so important: "Do your best to present yourself to God as one approved, a worker who has no need to be ashamed, rightly handling the word of truth."[94] A Christian soldier can wield his

---

[91] Norman L. Geisler and William E. Nix: *A General Introduction to the Bible* (Chicago, Moody Press, 1980), 367. (Emphasis is mine.)

[92] *Jewish Antiquities*, I, 146 [vi, 4].

[93] Merriam-Webster, Inc: *Merriam-Webster's Collegiate Dictionary*. Eleventh ed. (Springfield, Mass.: Merriam-Webster, Inc. 2003).

[94] Be diligent. This word denotes zealous persistence in accomplishing a goal. Timothy, like all who preach or teach the Word, was to give his maximum effort to impart God's Word completely, accurately, and clearly to his hearers. This is crucial to counter the disastrous effects of false teaching (vv. 14, 16, 17).–MacArthur, John (2005-05-09). *The*

weapons ("the sword of the Spirit") effectively in warfare only if he has practiced and has learned to use them well.

Ephesians 2:8-9 English Standard Version (ESV)

8 For by grace you have been saved through faith. And this is not your own doing; it is the gift of God, **9** not a result of works, so that no one may boast.

James 2:26 English Standard Version (ESV)

26 For as the body apart from the spirit is dead, so also faith apart from works is dead.

So, which is it? Is salvation possible by faith alone as Paul wrote to the Ephesians, or is faith dead without works as James wrote to his readers? As our subtitle brings out, let us look at the context. In the letter to the Ephesians, the apostle Paul is speaking to the Jewish Christians who were looking to the works of the Mosaic Law as a means to salvation, a righteous standing before God. Paul was telling these legalistic Jewish Christians that this is not so. In fact, this would invalidate Christ's ransom, because there would have been no need for it if one could achieve salvation by meticulously keeping the Mosaic Law. (Rom. 5:18) But James was writing to those in a congregation who were concerned with their status before other men, who were looking for prominent positions within the congregation, and not taking care of those that were in need. (Jam. 2:14–17) So, James is merely addressing those who call themselves Christian, but in name only. No person could truly be a Christian and not possess some good works, such as feeding the poor, helping the elderly. This type of work was an evident demonstration of one's Christian personality. Paul was in perfect harmony with James on this. – Romans 10:10; 1 Corinthians 15:58; Ephesians 5:15, 21–33; 6:15; 1 Timothy 4:16; 2 Timothy 4:5; Hebrews 10:23-25.

Inerrancy: Are There Contradictions?

Below I will follow this pattern. I will list the critic's argument first, followed by the text of difficulty, and conclude with an answer to the critic. What should be kept at the forefront of our mind is this: one is simply looking for the best answer, not absoluteness. If there is a reasonable answer to a Bible difficulty, why are the critics able to set them

MacArthur Bible Commentary (Kindle Locations 60689-60691). Thomas Nelson. Kindle Edition.

aside with ease? Because they start with the premise that this is not the Word of God, but only a book by imperfect men and full of contradictions; thus, the bias toward errors has blinded their judgment.

Critic: The critic would argue that there was an Adam and Eve, and an Abel who was now dead, so, where did Cain get his wife? This is one of the most common questions by Bible critics. Sadly, even though the answer has been around for 150 years and given by dozens of apologist, it is still used.

Genesis 4:17 New English Translation (NET Bible)

17 Cain had marital relations with his wife, and she became pregnant and gave birth to Enoch. Cain was building a city, and he named the city after his son Enoch.

Answer: If one were to read a little further along, they would come to the realization that Adam had a son named Seth; it further adds that Adam "became father to sons *and daughters*." (Genesis 5:4) Adam lived for a total of 800 years after fathering Seth, giving him ample opportunity to father many more sons and daughters. So it could be that Cain married one of his sisters. If he waited until one of his brothers and sisters had a daughter, he could have married one of his nieces once she was old enough. In the beginning, humans were closer to perfection; this explains why they lived longer and why at that time there was little health risk of genetic defects in the case of children born to closely related parents, in contrast to how it is today. As time passed, genetic defects increased and life spans decreased. Adam lived to see 930 years. Yet Shem, who lived after the Flood, died at 600 years, while Shem's son Arpachshad only lived 438 years, dying before his father died. Abraham saw an even greater decrease in that he only lived 175 years, while his grandson Jacob was 147 years when he died. Thus, due to increasing imperfection, God prohibited the marriage of closely related people under the Mosaic Law because of the likelihood of genetic defects.—Leviticus 18:9.

Critic: If God is here hardening Pharaoh's heart, what exactly makes Pharaoh responsible for the decisions he makes?

Exodus 4:21 Revised Standard Version (RSV)

21 And the Lord said to Moses, "When you go back to Egypt, see that you do before Pharaoh all the miracles which I have put in your power; but I will harden his heart, so that he will not let the people go.

Answer: This is actually a prophecy. God knew that what he was about to do would contribute to a stubborn and obstinate Pharaoh, who was going to be unwilling to change or give up the Israelites so they could go off to worship their God. Therefore, this is not stating what God is going to do; it is prophesying that Pharaoh's heart will harden because of the actions of God. The fact is, Pharaoh allowed his own heart to harden because he was determined not to agree with Moses' wishes or accept Jehovah's request to let the people go. Moses tells us at Exodus 7:13 (ESV) that "Pharaoh's heart was hardened, and he would not listen to them, as the Lord had said." Again, at 8:15 we read, "When Pharaoh saw that there was a respite, he hardened his heart and would not listen to them, as the Lord had said."

Critic: The Israelites had just received the Ten Commandments, with one commandment being: "You shall not make for yourself a carved image, or any likeness of anything that is in heaven above, or that is in the earth beneath, or that is in the water under the earth." Therefore, how is the bronze serpent not a violation of this commandment? Again, we will see that if the Christian reader just took a moment to investigated, there are reasonable and logical answers for thousands of Bible difficulties.

Numbers 21:9 English Standard Version (ESV)

9 So Moses made a bronze serpent and set it on a pole. And if a serpent bit anyone, he would look at the bronze serpent and live.

Answer: First, an idol is "a representation or symbol of an object of worship; *broadly*: a false god."[95] Second, it should be noted that not all images are idols. The bronze serpent was not made for the purpose of worship, or for some passionate devotion or veneration. There were times, however, when images were created with absolutely no intention of it receiving devotion, veneration, or worship, yet were later made into objects of veneration. That is exactly what happened with the copper serpent that Moses had formed in the wilderness. Many centuries later, "in the third year of Hoshea son of Elah, king of Israel, Hezekiah the son of Ahaz, king of Judah, began to reign. He removed the high places and broke the pillars and cut down the Asherah. And he broke in pieces the bronze serpent that Moses had made; for until those days the people of Israel had made offerings to it (it was called Nehushtan)."—2 Kings 18:1, 4.

Critic: Deuteronomy 15:11 (NET) says: "*There will never cease to be some poor people in the land*; therefore, I am commanding you to make

---

[95] Merriam-Webster, Inc: *Merriam-Webster's Collegiate Dictionary*. Eleventh ed. (Springfield, Mass.: Merriam-Webster, Inc., 2003).

sure you open your hand to your fellow Israelites who are needy and poor in your land." Is this not a contradiction of Deuteronomy 15:4? Will there be no poor among the Israelites, or will there be poor among them? Which is it?

Deuteronomy 15:4 New English Translation (NET Bible)

⁴ However, there should not be any poor among you, for the Lord will surely bless you in the land that he is giving you as an inheritance,

Answer: If you look at the context, Deuteronomy 15:4 is stating that if the Israelites obey Jehovah's command to take care of the poor, "there should not be any poor among" them. Thus, for every poor person, there will be one to take care of that need. If an Israelite fell on hard times, there was to be a fellow Israelite ready to step in to help him through those hard times. Verse 11 stresses the truth of the imperfect world since the rebellion of Adam and inherited sin: there will always be poor among mankind, the Israelites being no different. However, the difference with God's people is that those who were well off were to offset conditions for those who fell on difficult times. This is not to be confused with the socialistic welfare systems in the world today. Those Jews were hard-working men, who labored from sunup to sundown to take care of their families. But if disease overtook their herd or unseasonal weather brought about failed crops, an Israelite could sell himself into the service of a fellow Israelite for a period of time; thereafter, he would be back on his feet. And many years down the road, he may very well do the same for another Israelite who fell on difficult times.

Critic: Joshua 11:23[96] says that Joshua took the land according to what God had spoken to Moses and handed it on to the nation of Israel as planned. However, in Joshua 13:1, God is telling Joshua that he has grown old and much of the Promised Land has yet to be taken possession of. How can both be true? Is this not a contradiction? Many times at first glance, what seems like a contradiction is no such thing at all. We just have to trust the Word of God and take the time to investigate further with good conservative study tools. Keep in mind, not all study tools are

---

[96] **the whole land**. Here is a key summary verse for the whole book, which also sums up 11:16–22. How does this relate to 13:1, where God tells Joshua that he did not take the whole land? It may mean that the major battles had been fought and supremacy demonstrated, even if further incidents would occur and not every last pocket of potential resistance had yet been rooted out.–MacArthur, John (2005-05-09). *The MacArthur Bible Commentary* (Kindle Locations 10043-10045). Thomas Nelson. Kindle Edition.

equal. Many are not aware but there are very few truly conservative authors. As we draw near the end of Satan's evil rule, it seems that there is a separation of those, who are doing the will of the Father and those, who are doing their will. To the latter Jesus will say, "'I never knew you; depart from me, you workers of lawlessness.'"—Matthew 7:21-23, ESV.

Joshua 11:23 English Standard Version (ESV)

²³ So Joshua took the whole land, according to all that the Lord had spoken to Moses. And Joshua gave it for an inheritance to Israel according to their tribal allotments. And the land had rest from war.

Joshua 13:1 English Standard Version (ESV)

13 Now Joshua was old and advanced in years, and the Lord said to him, "You are old and advanced in years, and there remains yet very much land to possess.

Answer: No, it is not a contradiction. When the Israelites were to take the land, it was to take place in two different stages: the nation as a whole was to go to war and defeat the 31 kings of this land; thereafter, each Israelite tribe was to take their part of the land based on their individual actions. (Joshua 17:14–18; 18:3) Joshua fulfilled his role, which is expressed in 11:23, while the individual tribes did not complete their campaigns, which is expressed in 13:1. Even though the individual tribes failed to live up to taking their portion, the remaining Canaanites posed no real threat. Joshua 21:44, *ASV*, reads, "Jehovah gave them rest round about."

Critic: The critic would point out that John 1:18 clearly says, "*no one has ever seen God,*" while Exodus 24:10 explicitly states that Moses and Aaron, Nadab and Abihu, and seventy of the elders of Israel "*saw the God of Israel.*" Worse still, God informs them in Exodus 33:20: "You cannot see my face, for man shall not see me and live." The critic with his knowing smile says, 'This is a blatant contradiction.' The critic has offered the same old tired contradiction arguments for centuries, even though there have long been answers. They are depending on our being too lazy to look. Clearly, the reader of this book has decided that they are going to buy out the time, to know the issues raised and the answers that have long been available. Today, we have hundreds of great apologetic books to help us defend the Word of God against the atheistic Bible critics, who have taken on an evangelistic life, to decimate and destroy Christianity by lies and half-truths. Now, let us answer this so-called Bible difficulty, which they have raised and we have long answered.

John 1:18 New American Standard Bible (NASB)

[18] No one has seen God at any time; the only begotten God who is in the bosom of the Father, He has explained *Him*.[97]

Exodus 24:10 New American Standard Bible (NASB)

[10] and they saw the God of Israel; and under His feet there appeared to be a pavement of sapphire, as clear as the sky itself.

Exodus 33:20 English Standard Version (ESV)

[20] But," he [God] said, "you cannot see my face, for man shall not see me and live."

Answer: Exodus 33:20 is one-hundred percent correct: No human could see Jehovah God and live. The apostle Paul at Colossians 1:15 tell us that Christ is the image of the invisible God, and the writer informs us at Hebrews 1:3 that Jesus is the "exact representation of His nature." Yet if you were to read the account of Saul of Tarsus (the apostle Paul), you would see that a mere partial manifestation of Christ's glory blinded Saul – Acts 9:1–18.

When the Bible says that Moses and others have seen God, it is not speaking of *literally* seeing him, because first of all He is an invisible spirit person. It is a *manifestation* of his glory, which is an act of showing or demonstrating his presence, making himself perceptible to the human mind. In fact, it is generally an angelic representative that stands in his place and not him personally. Exodus 24:16 informs us that "the glory of the Lord dwelt on Mount Sinai," not the Lord himself personally. When texts such as Exodus 24:10 explicitly state that Moses and Aaron, Nadab and Abihu, and seventy of the elders of Israel "*saw the God of Israel*," it is this "glory of the Lord," an angelic representative. This is shown to be the case at Luke 2:9, which reads: "And *an angel of the Lord* appeared to them, and *the glory of the Lord shone around them* [the shepherds], and they were filled with fear."

---

[97] **1:17, 18** Corroborating the truth of verse 14, these verses draw a closing contrast to the prologue. The Law, given by Moses, was not a display of God's grace but God's demand for holiness. God designed the Law as a means to demonstrate the unrighteousness of man in order to show the need for a Savior, Jesus Christ (Rom. 3:19, 20; Gal. 3:10–14, 21–26). Furthermore, the Law revealed only a part of truth and was preparatory in nature. The reality or full truth toward which the Law pointed came through the person of Jesus Christ.– MacArthur, John (2005-05-09). The MacArthur Bible Commentary (Kindle Locations 46215-46218). Thomas Nelson. Kindle Edition.

Many Bible difficulties are cleared up elsewhere in Scripture; for example, in the New Testament you will find a text clarifying a difficulty from the Old Testament, such as Acts 7:53, which refers to those "who received the law *as delivered by angels* and did not keep it." Support comes from Paul at Galatians 3:19: "Why then the law? It was added because of transgressions, until the offspring should come to whom the promise had been made, and it was put in place through angels by an intermediary." The writer of Hebrews chimes in at 2:2 with "For since the message *declared by angels* proved to be reliable, and every transgression or disobedience received a just retribution. . . ." As we travel back to Exodus again, to 19:19 specifically, we find support that it was not God's own voice, which Moses heard; no, it was an angelic representative, for it reads: "Moses was speaking and God was answering him with a voice." Exodus 33:22–23 also helps us to appreciate that it was the back of these angelic representatives of Jehovah that Moses saw: "While my glory passes by . . . Then I will take away my hand, and you shall see my back, but my face shall not be seen."

Exodus 3:4 states: "God called to him out of the bush, 'Moses, Moses!' And he said, 'Here I am.'" Verse 6 informs us: "I am the God of your father, the God of Abraham, the God of Isaac, and the God of Jacob." Yet, in verse 2 we read: "And the angel of the Lord appeared to him in a flame of fire out of the midst of a bush." Here is another example of using God's Word to clear up what seems to be unclear or difficult to understand at first glance. Thus, while it speaks of the Lord making a direct appearance, it is really an angelic representative. Even today, we hear such comments, as 'the president of the United States is to visit the Middle East later this week.' However, later in the article it is made clear that he is not going personally, but it is one of his high-ranking representatives. Let us close with two examples, starting with,

Genesis 32:24-30 English Standard Version (ESV)

24 And Jacob was left alone. And a man wrestled with him until the breaking of the day. **25** When the man saw that he did not prevail against Jacob, he touched his hip socket, and Jacob's hip was put out of joint as he wrestled with him.**26** Then he said, "Let me go, for the day has broken." But Jacob said, "I will not let you go unless you bless me." **27** And he said to him, "What is your name?" And he said, "Jacob."**28** Then he said," Your name shall no longer be called Jacob, but Israel, for you have striven with God and with men, and have prevailed."**29** Then Jacob asked him, "Please tell me your name?" But he said, "Why is it that you ask my name?" And there he blessed him. **30** So

Jacob called the name of the place Peniel, saying, "For I have seen God face to face, and yet my life has been delivered."

It is all too obvious here that this man is simply a materialized angel in the form of a man, another angelic representative of Jehovah God. Moreover, the reader of this book should have taken in that the Israelites as a whole saw these angelic representatives, and spoke of them as though they were dealing directly with Jehovah God himself.

This proved to be the case in the second example found in the book of Judges where an angelic representative visited Manoah and his wife. Like the above mentioned account, Manoah and his wife treated this angelic representative as if he were Jehovah God himself: "And Manoah said to the angel of the Lord, 'What is your name, so that, when your words come true, we may honor you?' And the angel of the Lord said to him, 'Why do you ask my name, seeing it is wonderful?' Then Manoah knew that he was the angel of the Lord. And Manoah said to his wife, "We shall surely die, *for we have seen God*." – Judges 13:3–22.

Inerrancy: Are There Mistakes?

I have addressed the alleged contradictions, so it would seem that our job is done here, right? Not hardly. Yes, there are just as many who claim that the Bible is full of mistakes.

Critic: Matthew 27:5 states that Judas hanged himself, whereas Acts 1:18 says that "falling headlong he burst open in the middle and all his bowels gushed out." Is this a contradiction? Did Matthew or Luke make a mistake?

Matthew 27:5 English Standard Version (ESV)

5 And throwing down the pieces of silver into the temple, he departed, and he went and hanged himself.

Acts 1:18 English Standard Version (ESV)

18 (Now this man acquired a field with the reward of his wickedness, and falling headlong he burst open in the middle and all his bowels gushed out.

Answer: Neither Matthew, nor Luke made a mistake. What you have is Matthew giving the reader the manner in which Judas committed suicide. On the other hand, Luke is giving the reader of Acts, the result of that suicide. Therefore, instead of a mistake, we have two texts that complement each other, really giving the reader the full picture. Judas came to a tree alongside a cliff that had rocks below. He tied the rope to a branch and the other end around his neck, and jumped over the edge of the cliff in an attempt at hanging himself. One of two things could have happened: (1) the limb broke plunging him to the rocks below, or (2) the rope broke with the same result, and he burst open onto the rocks below.

Critic: The apostle Paul made a mistake when he quotes how many people died.

Numbers 25:9 English Standard Version (ESV)

⁹ Nevertheless, those who died by the plague were twenty-four thousand.

1 Corinthians 10:8 English Standard Version (ESV)

⁸ We must not indulge in sexual immorality as some of them did, and twenty-three thousand fell in a single day.

Answer: We must keep in mind the above principle that we spoke of, the *Intended Meaning of the Writer*. We live in a far more precise age today, where specificity is highly important. However, we round large numbers off (even estimate) all the time: "there were 237,000 people in Time Square last night." The simplest answer is that the number of people slain was in between 23,000 and 24,000, and both writers rounded the number off. However, there is even another possibility, because the book of Numbers specifically speaks of "all the chiefs of the people" (25:4-5), which could account for the extra 1,000, which is mentioned in Numbers 24,000. Thus, you have the people killing the chiefs of the people and the plague killing the people. Therefore, both books are correct.

Critic: After 215 years in Egypt, the descendants of Jacob arrived at the Promised Land. As you recall they sinned against God and were sentenced to forty years in the wilderness. However, once they entered the Promised Land, they buried Joseph's bones "at Shechem, in the piece of land that *Jacob bought* from the sons of Hamor the father of Shechem," as stated at Joshua 24:32. Yet, when Stephen had to defend himself before the Jewish religious leaders, he said that Joseph was buried "in the tomb that *Abraham had bought* for a sum of silver from the sons of Hamor." Therefore, at once it appears that we have a mistake on the part of Stephen. If we have one mistake in the Bible, it can no longer be claimed that it is fully inerrant. However, we can have one or more Bible difficulties that have not been answered because we simply have not discovered evidence for them as of yet.

Acts 7:15-16 English Standard Version (ESV)

¹⁵ And Jacob went down into Egypt, and he died, he and our fathers,¹⁶ and they were carried back to Shechem and laid in the tomb⁹⁸ that Abraham had bought for a sum of silver from the sons of Hamor in Shechem.

Genesis 23:17-18 English Standard Version (ESV)

¹⁷ So the field of Ephron in Machpelah, which was to the east of Mamre, the field with the cave that was in it and all the trees that were in the field, throughout its whole area, was made over ¹⁸ to Abraham as a possession in the presence of the Hittites, before all who went in at the gate of his city.

Genesis 33:19 English Standard Version (ESV)

¹⁹ And from the sons of Hamor, Shechem's father, he [Jacob] bought for a hundred pieces of money the piece of land on which he had pitched his tent.

Joshua 24:32 English Standard Version (ESV)

³² As for the bones of Joseph, which the people of Israel brought up from Egypt, they buried them at Shechem, in the piece of land that Jacob bought from the sons of Hamor the father of Shechem for a hundred pieces of money. It became an inheritance of the descendants of Joseph.

Answer: If we look back to Genesis 12:6-7, we will find that Abraham's first stop after entering Canaan from Haran was Shechem. It is here that Jehovah told Abraham: "To your offspring I will give this land." At this point Abraham built an altar to Jehovah. It seems reasonable that Abraham would need to purchase this land that had not yet been given to his offspring. While it is true that the Old Testament does not mention this purchase, it is likely that Stephen would be aware of such by way of oral tradition. As Acts chapter seven demonstrates, Stephen had a wide-ranging knowledge of Old Testament history.

Later, Jacob would have had difficulty laying claim to the tract of land that his grandfather Abraham had purchased, because there would have been a new generation of inhabitants of Shechem. This would have

---

⁹⁸ **they were . . . laid in the tomb**. "They" refers to Joseph (Josh. 24:32) and his brothers, but not Jacob, who was buried in Abraham's tomb at Machpelah (Gen. 50:13).– MacArthur, John (2005-05-09). *The MacArthur Bible Commentary* (Kindle Locations 49379-49380). Thomas Nelson. Kindle Edition.

been many years after Abraham moved further south and Isaac moved to Beersheba, and including Jacob's twenty years in Paddan-aram (Gen 28:6, 7). The simplest answer is that this land was not in use for about 120 years because of Abraham's extensive travels and Isaac's having moved away, leaving it unused; likely it was put to use by others. So, Jacob simply repurchased what Abraham had bought over a hundred years earlier. This is very similar to the time Isaac had to repurchase the well at Beersheba that Abraham had already purchased earlier. – Genesis 21:27–30; 26:26–32.

Genesis 33:18–20 tells us that 'Jacob bought this land for a hundred pieces of money, from the sons of Hamor.' This same transaction is also mentioned at Joshua 24:32, in reference to transporting Joseph's bones from Egypt, to be buried in Shechem.

We should also address the cave of Machpelah that Abraham had purchased in Hebron from Ephron the Hittite. The word "tomb" is not mentioned until Joshua 24:32, and is in reference to the tract of land in Shechem. Nowhere in the Old Testament does it say that Abraham bought a "tomb." The cave of Machpelah obtained by Abraham would eventually become a family tomb, receiving Sarah's body and, eventually, his own, and those of Isaac, Rebekah, Jacob, and Leah. (Genesis 23:14–19; 25:9; 49:30, 31; 50:13) Gleason L. Archer, Jr., concludes this Bible difficulty, saying:

The reference to a *mnema* ("tomb") in connection with Shechem must either have been proleptic [to anticipate] for the later use of that shechemite tract for Joseph's tomb (i.e., 'the tomb that Abraham bought' was intended to imply 'the tomb location that Abraham bought"); or else conceivably the dative relative pronoun *ho* was intended elliptically [omission] for *en to topo ho onesato Abraam* ("in the place that Abraham bought") as describing the location of the *mnema* near the Oak of Moreh right outside Shechem. Normally Greek would have used the relative-locative adverb *hou* to express 'in which' or 'where'; but this would have left *onesato* ("bought") without an object in its own clause, and so *ho* was much more suitable in this context. (Archer 1982, 379–81)

Another solution could be that Jacob is being viewed as a representative of Abraham, for he is the grandson of Abraham. This was quite appropriate in Biblical times, to attribute the purchase to Abraham as the Patriarchal family head.

Critic: 2 Samuel 24:1 says that God moved David to count the Israelites, while 1 Chronicles 21:1 Satan, or a resister did. This would seem to be a clear mistake on the part of one of these authors.

2 Samuel 24:1 English Standard Version (ESV)

¹ Again the anger of the Lord was kindled against Israel, and he incited David against them, saying, "Go, number Israel and Judah."

1 Chronicles 21:1 English Standard Version (ESV)

¹ Then Satan stood against Israel and incited David to number Israel.

Answer: In this period of David's reign, Jehovah was very displeased with Israel, and therefore he did not prevent Satan from bringing this sin on them. Often in Scripture, it is spoken of as though God did something when he allowed an event to take place. For example, it is said that God 'hardened Pharaoh's heart' (Exodus 4:21), when he actually allowed the Pharaoh's heart to harden.

Inerrancy: Are There Scientific Errors?

Many truths about God are beyond the scope of science. Science and the Bible are not at odds. In fact, we can thank modern day science, as it has helped us to better under the creation of God, from our solar system, to the universes, to the human body and mind. What we find is a level of order, precision, design and sophistication, which points to a Designer, the eyes of many Christians, to an Almighty God, with infinite intelligence and power. The apostle Paul makes this all too clear, when he writes, "For his invisible attributes, namely, his eternal power and divine nature, have been clearly perceived, ever since the creation of the world, in the things that have been made. So they are without excuse." – Romans 1:20.

Back in the seventeenth century, the world-renowned scientist Galileo proved beyond any doubt that the earth was not the center of the universe, nor did the sun orbit the earth. In fact, he proved it to be the other way around (no pun intended), with the earth revolving around the sun. However, he was brought up on charges of heresy by the Catholic Church and ordered to recant his position. Why? From the viewpoint of the Catholic Church, Galileo was contradicting God's Word, the Bible. As it turned out, Galileo and science were correct and the Church was wrong, for which it issued a formal apology in 1992. However, the point we wish to make here is that in all the controversy, the Bible was never in the wrong. It was a misinterpretation on the part of the Catholic Church, and not a fault with the Bible. One will find no place in the Bible that claims the sun orbits the earth. So where would the Church get such an idea? The Church got such an idea from Ptolemy (b. about 85 C.E.), an ancient astronomer, who argued for such an idea.

As it usually turns out, the so-called contradiction between science and God's Word lies at the feet of those who are interpreting Scripture incorrectly. To repeat the sentiments of Galileo when writing to a pupil—Galileo expressed the same sentiments: "Even though Scripture cannot err, its interpreters and expositors can, in various ways. One of these, very serious and very frequent, would be when they always want to stop at the purely literal sense."[99] I believe that today's scholars, in hindsight, would have no problem agreeing.

While the Bible is not a science textbook, it is scientifically accurate when it touches on matters of science.

The Circle of the Earth Hangs on Nothing

Isaiah 40:22 English Standard Version (ESV)

22 It is he who sits above **the circle of the earth**,
and its inhabitants are like grasshoppers;
who stretches out the heavens like a curtain,
and spreads them like a tent to dwell in;

More than 2,500 years ago, the prophet Isaiah wrote that the earth is a circle or sphere. First, how would it be possible for Isaiah to know the earth is a circle or sphere, if not from inspiration? Scientific America writes, "As countless photos from space can attest, Earth is round—the "Blue Marble," as astronauts have affectionately dubbed it. Appearances, however, can be deceiving. Planet Earth is not, in fact, perfectly round."[100] Scientifically speaking, the sun is not perfectly, absolutely 100 percent round but in everyday speech, this verse is both acceptable and accurate, when we keep in mind it is written from a human perspective, not from a scientific perspective. Moreover, Isaiah was not discussing astronomy; he was simply making an inspired observation that man came to realize once he was in space, looking back at the earth, it is round. See the section about title, "Intended Meaning of Writer."

---

[99] Letter from Galileo to Benedetto Castelli, December 21, 1613.

[100] Charles Q. Choi (April 12, 2007). Scientific America. Strange but True: Earth Is Not Round. Retrieved Monday, August 03, 2015.

http://www.scientificamerican.com/article/earth-is-not-round/

Job 26:7 English Standard Version (ESV)

⁷ He stretches out the north over the void
and hangs the earth on nothing.

Here the author describes the earth as hanging upon nothing. Many have never heard of the Greek mathematician and astronomer Eratosthenes. He was born in about 276 B.C.E. and received some of his education in Athens, Greece. In 240 B.C., the "Greek astronomer, geographer, mathematician and librarian Eratosthenes calculates the Earth's circumference. His data was rough, but he wasn't far off."[101] While man very early on used their God given intelligence to arrive at some outstanding conclusion that were actually very accurate, we learn two points here. Eratosthenes was a very astute scientist, while Isaiah, who wrote some 500 years earlier, was no scientist at all. Moreover, Moses, who wrote the book of Job over 1,230 years before Eratosthenes, knew that the earth hung upon nothing.

How Is the Sun Standing Still Possible?

Joshua 10:13 English Standard Version (ESV)

¹³And the sun stood still, and the moon stopped, until the nation took vengeance on their enemies.

The Canaanites had besieged the Gibeonites, a group of people that gained Jehovah God's backing because they had faith in Him. In this battle, Jehovah helped the Israelites continue their attack by causing "the sun [to stand] still, and the moon stopped, until the nation took vengeance on their enemies." (Jos 10:1-14) Those who accept God as the creator of the universe and life can accept that he would know a way of stopping the earth from rotating. However, there are other ways of understanding this account. We must keep in mind that the Bible speaks from an earthly observer point of view, so it need not be that he stopped the rotation. It could have been a refraction of solar and lunar light rays, which would have produced the same effect.

Psalm 136:6 English Standard Version (ESV)

---

[101] Alfred, Randy (June 19, 2008). "June 19, 240 B.C.E: The Earth Is Round, and It's This Big". Wired. Retrieved Monday, August 03, 2015.

[6]to him who spread out the earth above the waters, for his steadfast love endures forever;[102]

Hebrews 3:4 English Standard Version (ESV)

[4](For every house is built by someone, but the builder of all things is God.)

2 Kings 20:8-11 English Standard Version (ESV)

[8]And Hezekiah said to Isaiah, "What shall be the sign that the LORD will heal me, and that I shall go up to the house of the LORD on the third day?" [9]And Isaiah said, "This shall be the sign to you from the LORD, that the LORD will do the thing that he has promised: shall the shadow go forward ten steps, or go back ten steps?" [10]And Hezekiah answered, "It is an easy thing for the shadow to lengthen ten steps. Rather let the shadow go back ten steps." [11]And Isaiah the prophet called to the LORD, and he brought the shadow back ten steps, by which it had gone down on the steps of Ahaz.

How is it that the stars fought on behalf of Barak?

Judges 5:20 English Standard Version (ESV)

[20] From heaven the stars fought, from their courses they fought against Sisera.

Judges 4:15 English Standard Version (ESV)

[15] And the LORD routed Sisera and all his chariots and all his army before Barak by the edge of the sword. And Sisera got down from his chariot and fled away on foot.

In the Bible, you have Biblical prose, and Biblical poetry.

Prose: language that is not poetry: (1) writing or speech in its normal continuous form, without the rhythmic or visual line structure of poetry **(2)** ordinary style of expression: writing or speech that is ordinary or matter-of-fact, without embellishment.

Poetry: literature in verse: (1) literary works written in verse, in particular verse writing of high quality, great beauty, emotional sincerity

---

[102] 139:6. David's response to all this is, Such knowledge is too wonderful and too high. God's omniscience is both convicting and comforting. For David, it was humbling, beyond his human capacity to grasp.–Anders, Max; Lawson, Steven (2006-04-01). *Holman Old Testament Commentary - Psalms 76-150* (Kindle Locations 8148-8149). B&H Publishing. Kindle Edition.

or intensity, or profound insight **(2) beauty or grace:** something that resembles poetry in its beauty, rhythmic grace, or imaginative, elevated, or decorative style.

We have a beautiful example of both of these forms of writing-communication in chapters four and five of the book of Judges. Judges Chapter 4 is a prose account of Deborah and Barak, while Judges Chapter 5 is a poetic account. As we have learned from the above, poetry is less concerned with accuracy than evoking emotions. Poetry has a license to say things like what we find in of 5:20, which is in the poetry chapter: "from heaven the stars fought." This can be said and the reader is expected to not take the language literally. What we can surmise from it though, is that God was acting against Sisera in some way, there was divine intervention.

Procedures for Handling Bible Difficulties

1. You need to be completely convinced a reason or understanding exists.

2. You need to have total trust and conviction in the inerrancy of the Scripture as originally written down.

3. You need to study the context and framework of the verse carefully, to establish what the author meant by the words he used. In other words, find the beginning and the end of the context that your passage falls within.

4. You need to understand exegesis: find the historical setting, determine author intent, study key words, and note parallel passages. You need to slow down and carefully read the account, considering exactly what is being said

5. You need to find a reasonable harmonization of parallel passages.

6. You need to consider a variety of trusted Bible commentaries, dictionaries, lexical sources, encyclopedias, as well as books on Bible difficulties.

7. You should investigate as to whether the difficulty is a transmissional error in the original text.

8. You must always keep in mind that the historical accuracy of the biblical text is unmatched; that thousands of extant manuscripts some of

which date back to the second century B.C. support the transmitted text of Scripture.

9. We must keep in mind that the Bible is a diverse book when it comes to literary styles: narrative, poetic, prophetic, and apocalyptic; also containing parables, metaphors, similes, hyperbole, and other figures of speech. Too often, these alleged errors are the result of a reader taking a figure of speech as literal, or reading a parable as though it is a narrative.

10. The Bible student needs to understand what level that the Bible intends to be exact in what is written. If Jim told a friend that 650 graduated with him from high school in 1984, it is not challenged, because it is all too clear that he is using rounded numbers and is not meaning to be precise.

Review Question

- Can the Bible be trusted? Explain.

- What are some practical principles for overcoming Bible difficulties?

- Are there contradictions in the Bible? Explain.

- Are there mistakes in the Bible? Explain.

- Are there scientific errors in the Bible? Explain.

- What are some procedures for handling Bible difficulties

APPENDIX C 10 Dealing With Bible Difficulties

By R. A. Torrey

Updated and Expanded by Edward D. Andrews

Before taking up those specific difficulties and alleged "contradictions" in the Bible, which have caused the most trouble to seekers after truth, let us first consider how difficulties should be dealt with.

Honestly

Whenever you find a difficulty in the Bible frankly, acknowledge it. Do not try to obscure it. Do not try to dodge it. Look it square in the face. Admit it frankly to whoever mentions it. If you cannot give a good, square, honest explanation, do not attempt any at all. Those, who in their zeal for the infallibility of the Bible have attempted explanations of difficulties that do not commend themselves to the honest, fair-minded man, have done untold harm. People have concluded that if these are the best explanations, then there are really no explanations at all, and the Bible instead of being helped has been injured by the unintelligent zeal of foolish friends. If you are not really convinced that the Bible is the Word of God, you can far better afford to wait for an honest solution of a difficulty than you can afford to attempt a solution that is evasive and unsatisfactory.

Humbly

Recognize the limitations of your own mind and knowledge, and do not for a moment imagine that there is no solution just because you have found none. There is, in all probability, a very simple solution, even when you can find no solution at all.

Determinedly

Make up your mind that you will find the solution if you can by any amount of study and hard thinking. The difficulties of the Bible are our heavenly Father's challenge to us to set our brains to work. Do not give up searching for a solution because you cannot find it in five minutes or ten minutes. Ponder over it and work over it for days if necessary. The work will be more beneficial than the solution does. There is a solution somewhere, and you will find it if you will only search for it long enough and hard enough.

Fearlessly

Do not be frightened when you find a difficulty, no matter how unanswerable or how insurmountable it appears at first sight. Thousands of men have encountered just such difficulties, and still the old Book has withstood the test of time, being the bestseller that will never be touch, in the untold billions of copies. The Bible that has stood eighteen centuries of rigid examination, and of incessant and awful assault, is not likely to go down before your discoveries or before the discharges of any modern critical guns. To one who is at all familiar with the history of critical attacks on the Bible, the confidence of those modern critics who think they are going to annihilate the Bible at last is simply amusing.

Patiently

Do not be discouraged because you do not solve every problem in a day. If some difficulty persistently defies your very best efforts at a solution, lay it aside for a while. Later it will likely be resolved, and you will wonder how you were ever perplexed by it.

Scripturally

If you find a difficulty in one part of the Bible, look for another scripture to throw light upon it and dissolve it. Nothing explains scripture like scripture. Repeatedly people have come to me with some difficulty in the Bible that had greatly staggered them, and asked for a solution. I have been able to give a solution by simply asking them to read some other chapter and verse, and the simple reading of that scripture has thrown such light upon the passage in question that all the mists have disappeared and the truth has shone as clear as day.

Prayerfully

It is simply wonderful how difficulties dissolve when one looks at them on his knees. Not only does God open our eyes in answer to prayer to behold wonderful things out of His law, but He also opens our eyes to look straight through a difficulty that seemed impenetrable before we prayed. One great reason why many modern Bible scholars have learned to be destructive critics is because they have forgotten how to pray.

Review Question

- What are some ways that we can deal with Bible difficulties?

APPENDIX D View of Bible Difficulties

By R. A. Torrey

Updated By Edward D. Andrews

Every careful student and every thoughtful reader of the Bible finds that the words of the Apostle Peter concerning the Scriptures, that there are some things in them hard to be understood is true. The apostle Peter says of Paul's letters, "as *he does* also in all his [Paul's] letters, speaking in them about these *things*, in which there are some *things* **hard to understand**, which the ignorant and unstable distort to their own destruction, as *they* also *do* the rest of the scriptures." (2 Peter 3:16, LEB) If this were true of Peter, how much more so of us 2,000 years removed, of a different language and culture? This is abundantly true for us! Who of us has not found things in the Bible that have puzzled us, yes, that in our early Christian experience have led us to question whether the Bible was, after all, the Word of God? We find some things in the Bible, which it seems impossible to reconcile with other things in the Bible. We find some things which seem incompatible with the thought that the whole Bible is of divine origin and absolutely inerrant.

It is not wise to attempt to conceal the fact that these difficulties exist. It is the part of wisdom, as well as of honesty, to frankly face them and consider them.

What shall we say concerning these difficulties that every thoughtful student will eventually encounter?

The first thing we have to say about these difficulties in the Bible is that from the very nature of the case *difficulties are to be expected.*

Some people are surprised and staggered because there are difficulties in the Bible. For my part, I would be more surprised and staggered if there were not. What is the Bible? It is a revelation of the mind and will and character and being of an infinitely great, perfectly wise and absolutely holy God. God Himself is the Author of this revelation. However, one would ask, to who specifically is the revelation made? To men, to finite beings who are imperfect in intellectual development and consequently in knowledge, and who are imperfect in character and consequently in spiritual discernment. The wisest man measured on the scale of eternity is only a babe, and the holiest man compared with God is only an infant in moral development. Therefore, there must from the very necessities of the case, be difficulties in such a revelation from such a source made to such persons. In addition, when the finite are attempting to understand the infinite, there is bound to be difficulty. When the ignorant contemplate the utterances of one perfect in knowledge, there must be many things hard to be understood, and some things, which to their immature and inaccurate minds appear absurd. When beings whose moral judgments as to the hatefulness of sin and as to the awfulness of the penalty that it demands, listen to the demands of an absolutely holy Being, they are bound to be staggered at some of His demands; and when they consider His dealings, they are bound to be staggered at some of His dealings. These dealings will appear too severe, too stern, and too harsh.

It is plain that there must be difficulties for us in such a revelation as the Bible has proved to be. If someone should hand me a book that was as simple to me as the multiplication table, and say, "This is the Word of God; in it He has revealed His whole will and wisdom," I should shake my head and say, "I cannot believe it; that is too easy to be a perfect revelation of infinite wisdom." There must be in any complete revelation of God's mind and will and character and being, things hard for the beginner to understand; and the wisest and best of us are but beginners.

The second thing to be said about these difficulties is that a difficulty in a doctrine, or a grave objection to a doctrine, does not in any way prove the doctrine to be untrue.

Many people think that it does. If they come across some difficulty in the way of believing in the divine origin and absolute inerrancy and infallibility of the Bible, they at once conclude that the doctrine is exploded. That is very illogical. They should stop a moment and think, and learn to be reasonable and fair.

There is scarcely a doctrine in science generally believed today, that has not had some great difficulty in the way of its acceptance.

When the Copernican theory (the earth revolves around the sun and not vice versa), now so universally accepted, was first proclaimed, it encountered a very grave difficulty. If this theory were true, the planet Venus should have phases as the moon has, but no phases could be discovered by the best glass then in existence. However, the positive argument for the theory was so strong that it was accepted in spite of this apparently unanswerable objection. When a more powerful glass was made, it was found that Venus had phases after all. The whole difficulty arose, as most; all of those in the Bible arise, from man's ignorance of some of the facts in the case.

The nebular hypothesis (the formation of the solar system) is commonly accepted in the scientific world today. Nevertheless, when this theory was first announced, and for a long time afterward, the movements of the planet Uranus could not be reconciled with the theory. Uranus seemed to move in just the opposite direction from that in which it was thought it ought to move in accordance with the demands of the theory. However, the positive arguments for the theory were so strong that it was accepted in spite of the inexplicable movements of Uranus.

If we apply to Bible study the commonsense logic recognized in every department of science (with the exception of Biblical criticism, if that be a science), then we must demand that if the positive proof of a theory is conclusive, it must be believed by rational men in spite of any number of difficulties in minor details. He is a shallow thinker who gives up a well-attested truth because there are some apparent facts, which he cannot reconcile with that truth. In addition, he is a very shallow Bible scholar who gives up his belief in the divine origin and inerrancy of the Bible because there are some supposed facts that he cannot reconcile with that doctrine. There are in the theological world today many shallow thinkers of that kind.

The third thing to be said about the difficulties in the Bible is: there are many more, and much greater, difficulties in the way of the doctrine that holds the Bible to be of human origin, and hence fallible, than there are in the way of the doctrine that holds the Bible to be of divine origin, and hence infallible.

Turning the Tables

Oftentimes a man will put forth some difficulty and say, "How do you explain that, if the Bible is the Word of God?" You may not be able to answer him satisfactorily. Then he thinks he has you cornered. Not at all, turn on him, and ask him, "How do you account for the fulfilled prophecies of the Bible if it is of human origin? How do you account for the marvelous unity of the Book? How do you account for its inexhaustible depth? How do you account for its unique power in lifting men up to God?" For every insignificant objection he can bring to your view of the Bible, you can bring very many more deeply significant objections to his view of the Bible. Moreover, any candid man who desires to know and obey the truth will have no difficulty in deciding between the two views.

Some time ago a young man, who was of a bright mind and unusually well read in skeptical, critical, and agnostic literature, told me he had given the matter a great deal of candid and careful thought, and as a result he could not believe the Bible was of divine origin.

I asked him, "Why not?"

He pointed to a certain teaching of the Bible that he could not and would not believe to be true.

I replied, "Suppose for a moment that I could not answer that specific difficulty; that would not prove that the Bible is not of divine origin. I can bring you many things far more difficult to account for on the hypothesis that the Bible is not of divine origin than on the hypothesis that the Bible is of divine origin. You cannot deny the fact of fulfilled prophecy. How do you account for it if the Bible is not God's Word? You cannot shut eyes to the marvelous unity of the sixty-six books of the Bible, written under such divergent circumstances and at periods of time so remote from one another. How do you account for it if God is not the real Author of the Book back of the forty or more human authors? You cannot deny that the Bible has a power, to save men from sin, to bring men peace and hope and joy, to lift men up to God, that all other books taken together do not possess. How do you account for it if the Bible is not the Word of God in a sense that no other book is the Word of God?"

The objector did not answer. The difficulties that confront one who denies that the Bible is of divine origin and authority are far more numerous and vastly more weighty than those which confront the one who believes it to be of divine origin and authority.

The fourth thing to be said about the difficulties in the Bible is: *the fact that you cannot solve a difficulty does not prove it cannot be solved, and the fact that you cannot answer an objection does not prove at all that it cannot be answered.*

It is remarkable how often we overlook this very evident fact. There are many who, who meet a difficulty in the Bible and give it a little thought and can see no possible solution, at once jump at the conclusion that a solution is impossible, and so they give up their faith in the inerrancy of the Bible and in its divine origin. Any man should have a sufficient amount of modesty, being so limited in knowledge, to say, "Though I see no possible solution to this difficulty, someone a little wiser than I might easily find one."

If we would only bear in mind that we do not know everything, and there are a great many things that we cannot solve now which we could very easily solve if we only knew a little more, it would save us from all this foolishness. We ought never to forget that there may be a very easy solution to infinite wisdom even for that which to our finite wisdom, or ignorance, appears unsolvable. What would we think of a beginner in algebra who, having tried in vain for half an hour to solve a difficult problem, declared that there was no possible solution to the problem because he could find none!

A man of unusual experience and ability one day left his work and drove a long distance to see me, as he was in great uneasiness of mind because he had discovered what he believed to be a flat contradiction in the Bible. He had lain awake all night thinking about it. It had defied all his attempts at reconciliation, but when he had fully stated the case to me, in a very few moments I showed him a very simple and satisfactory solution of the difficulty. He went away with a happy heart. Nevertheless, why had it not occurred to him at the outset that, though it appeared impossible to him to find a solution, after all, someone else might easily discover a solution? He supposed that the difficulty was an entirely new one, but it was one that had been faced and answered long before either he or I were born.

The fifth thing to be said about the difficulties in the Bible is that *the seeming defects of the Book are exceedingly insignificant when put in comparison with its many and marvelous areas of excellence.*

It certainly reveals great perversity of both mind and heart that men spend so much time focusing on and exaggerating such insignificant points, which they consider defects in the Bible, and pass absolutely unnoticed the incomparable beauties and wonders that adorn and glorify almost every page. This is even taking place in some prominent institutions of learning, where men are supposed to be taught to appreciate and understand the Bible and where they are sent to be trained to preach its truth to others. These institutions are spending much more time on minute and insignificant points that seem to point toward an entirely human origin of the Bible than is spent upon studying and understanding and admiring the unparalleled glories that make this Book stand apart from all other books in the world. What would we think of any man who in studying some great masterpiece of art concentrated his whole attention upon what looked like a flyspeck in the corner? A large proportion of the much boasted about "critical study of the Bible" is a laborious and scholarly investigation of supposed flyspecks. The man who is **not** willing to squander the major portion of his time in this intellectualized investigation of flyspecks but prefers to devote it to the study of the unrivaled beauties and majestic splendors of the Book is counted in some quarters as not being "scholarly and up to date."

The sixth thing to be said about the difficulties in the Bible is that *they have far more weight with superficial readers than with profound students.*

Take a man like Colonel Ingersoll, who was very ignorant of the real contents and meaning of the Bible, or that class of modern preachers who read the Bible for the most part for the sole purpose of finding texts to serve as pegs to hang their own ideas. To such superficial readers of the Bible these difficulties seem of immense importance, but to one who has learned to meditate upon the Word of God day and night they have scarcely any weight at all. That rare man of God, George Müller, who had carefully studied the Bible from beginning to end more than one hundred times, was not disturbed by any difficulties he encountered; but to the man who is reading it through for the first or second time there are many things that perplex and stagger.

The seventh thing to be said about the difficulties in the Bible is that *they rapidly disappear upon careful and prayerful study.*

How many things there are in the Bible that once puzzled and staggered us, but which have since been perfectly cleared up and no longer present any difficulty whatever! Every year of study finds these difficulties disappear more and more rapidly. At first they go by ones, and then by twos, and then by dozens, and then by scores. Is it not reasonable then to suppose that the difficulties that remain will all disappear upon further study?

Review Question

- How have some reacted when they discovered there are Bible difficulties?

- How should we view Bible difficulties

- How can we turn the table on Bible critics?

APPENDIX E Some Types of Bible Difficulties

By R. A. Torrey

Updated by Edward D. Andrews

All the difficulties found in the Bible can be included under ten general headings:

The Text from which our English Bible was Translated

No one, as far as I know, holds that the English translation of the Bible is absolutely infallible and inerrant. The doctrine held by many is that the Scriptures as originally given were absolutely infallible and inerrant, and that our English translation is a *substantially accurate* rendering of the Scriptures as originally given.

We do not possess the original manuscripts of the Bible. These original manuscripts were copied many times with great care and exactness, but naturally, some errors crept into the copies that were made. We now possess so many good copies that by comparing one with another, we can tell with great precision just what the original text was. Indeed, for all practical purposes the original text is now settled.

Update: After Torrey's death in 1928, we have made the extremely important discovery over 100 papyrus manuscripts that date before 300 C.E. Quite a few date to the second century, with one small fragment being dated to about 125 C.E. The modern textual scholar can now say with certainty that we have establish the Greek New Testament to a ninety-nine percent reflect of the originally publish book(s). Moreover, we have more than 100 English translations today, with many of them being a very good representation of the Hebrew and Greek in English: NASB, ESB, HCSB, LEB, and others. **Edward D. Andrews**

There is not one important doctrine, which hangs upon any doubtful reading of the text. However, when our Authorized Version (KJV) was published in 1611, some of the best manuscripts were not within reach of the translators, and the science of textual criticism was not so well understood as it is today, and so the translation was made from an imperfect text. Not a few of the apparent difficulties in the Bible arise from this source.

For example, we are told in John 5:4 that "an angel went down at a certain season into the pool, and troubled the water: whosoever then first after the troubling of the water stepped in was made whole of whatsoever disease he had." This statement for many reasons seems improbable and difficult to believe, but upon investigation, we find that it is all a mistake of the copyist. Some early copyist, reading John's account, added in the margin his explanation of the healing properties of this intermittent medicinal spring. A late copyist embodied this marginal note in the body of the text, and so it came to be handed down and got into the Authorized Version (KJV). Very properly, it has been omitted from the Revised Version.

Note: It is omitted from almost all of our modern-day translations as well, with the exception of the NASB and the HCSB, which retained it out of esteem to the KJV. **Edward S. Andrews**

The discrepancies in figures in different accounts of the same events as, for example, the differences in the ages of some of the kings as given in the text of Kings and Chronicles, doubtless arise from the same cause, errors of copyists. Such an error in the matter of figures would be very easy to make, as in the Hebrew; letters, and letters that appear very much alike have a very different value as figures denote numbers. For example, the first letter in the Hebrew alphabet denotes one, and with two little points above it, no larger than flyspecks, it denotes a thousand. The twenty-third or last letter of the Hebrew alphabet denotes four hundred, but the eighth letter of the Hebrew alphabet that looks very much like it and could be easily mistaken for it, denotes eight. A very slight error of the copyist would therefore make an utter change in figures. The remarkable thing when one contemplates the facts in the case is that so few errors of this kind have been made.

Inaccurate Translations

For example, in Matthew 12:40 Jonah is spoken of as being in "the whale's belly." Many a skeptic has made a mockery over the thought of a whale with the peculiar construction of its mouth and throat swallowing a man. However, if the skeptic had only taken the trouble to look the matter up, he would have found the word translated "whale" really means "sea monster" [or great fish] without any definition as to the character of the sea monster. We will take this up more in detail in considering the story of Jonah. Therefore, the whole difficulty arose from the translator's mistake and the skeptic's ignorance. Many skeptics today are so densely ignorant of matters clearly understood by many Sunday school children that they are still harping in the name of scholarship on this supposed error in the Bible.

False Interpretations of the Bible

What the Bible teaches is one thing, and what men interpret it to mean is oftentimes something widely different. Many difficulties that we have with the Bible arise not from what the Bible actually says, but from what men interpret it to mean.

A striking illustration of this is found in Genesis 1. If we were to take the interpretation put upon this chapter by many, it would indeed be difficult to reconcile it with much that modern science regards as established. However, the difficulty is not with what Genesis 1 says, but with the interpretation put upon it. There is no contradiction whatever between what is really proven by science and what is really said in Genesis 1.

Another difficulty of the same character is with Jesus' statement that He would be three days and three nights in the heart of the earth. Many interpreters would have us believe that He died Friday and rose early Sunday morning, and the time between these two is far from being three days and three nights. However, it is a matter of biblical interpretation, and the trouble is not with what the Bible actually says, but with the interpretation that men put upon the Bible. We will take this matter up at length below by Edward D. Andrews.

Matthew 12:40 How many days was Jesus in the tomb?

Some argue for three days, based on Jesus' words,

Matthew 12:40 English Standard Version (ESV)

40 For just as Jonah was three days and three nights in the belly of the great fish, so will the Son of Man be three days and three nights in the heart of the earth.

This would seem to suggest a full 72 hours. However, we should not set aside similar expressions that may allow us to get at the intent of the words. Many times in Scripture, three days does not always mean a full 72 hours of three days. For example, look at the words of Reheboam,

1 Kings 12:5, 12 English Standard Version (ESV)

⁵ He said to them, "Go away for three days, then come again to me." So the people went away. ¹² So Jeroboam and all the people came to Rehoboam the third day, as the king said, "Come to me again the third day."

You see that the king told the people to go away for three days, and then return to him. But you als will notice that they returned on the third day, which was not a full 72 hours of three days. Now, consider what Jesus said of himself, something that Scripture repeatedly says,

Luke 24:46 English Standard Version (ESV)

⁴⁶ and said to them, "Thus it is written, that the Christ should suffer and **on the third day** rise from the dead

Now, if he had remained in the grave for a full 72 hours of three days, it mean that he would have been raised on the fourth day. Jewish days ran from sundown to sundown. Jesus died on Friday afternoon about 3:00 p.m., Nisan 14, 33 C.E.

- Jesus' death Friday Nisan 14, about 3:00 p.m. (Matt 27:31-56; Mk 15:20-41; Lu 23:26-49; Jn 19:16-30)

- Jesus was in Tomb before sundown Friday evening (Matt 27:57-61; Mk 15:42-47; Lu 23:50-56; Jn 19:31-42)

- Jesus in tomb all of Nisan 15ᵗʰ from sundown Friday to sundown Saturday, which began Nisan 16 (Matt 27:62-66)

- Jesus resurrected early Sunday morning of Nisan 16ᵗʰ (Matt 28:1; Mk 16:1; Lu 24:1; Jn 20:1)

Therefore, Jesus was dead and in the tomb for at least a period of time on Friday Nisan 14, was still in the tomb during the course of the whole day of Nisan 15, and spent the nighttime hours of Nisan 16 in the tomb.

- Now after the Sabbath, toward the dawn of the first day of the week, Mary Magdalene and the other Mary went to see the tomb. (Matt 28:1)

- When the Sabbath was past, Mary Magdalene, Mary the mother of James, and Salome bought spices, so that they might go and anoint him. (Mk 16:1)

- But on the first day of the week, at early dawn, they went to the tomb, taking the spices they had prepared. (Lu 24:1)

- Now on the first day of the week Mary Magdalene came to the tomb early, while it was still dark, and saw that the stone had been taken away from the tomb. (Jn 20:1)

Certain women came to the tomb on Sunday morning, it was still dark, he had already been resurrected. Thus, Jesus had been in the tomb for parts of three days.

A Wrong Conception of the Bible

Many think that when you say the Bible is the Word of God, of divine origin and authority, you mean that God is the speaker in every utterance it contains; but this is not at all, what is meant. Oftentimes it simply records what others say—what good men say, what bad men say, what inspired men say, what uninspired men say, what angels and demons say, and even what the devil says. The record of what they said is from God and absolutely true, but what those other persons are recorded as saying may be true or may not be true. It is true that they said it, but what they said may not be true.

For example, the devil is recorded in Genesis 3:4 as saying, "You will not surely die." It is true that the devil said it, but what the devil said is not true, but an infamous lie that shipwrecked our race. That the devil said it is God's Word, but what the devil said is not God's word but the devil's word. It is God's Word that this was the devil's word.

Very many careless readers of the Bible do not notice who is talking, God, good men, bad men, inspired men, uninspired men, angels or devil. They will tear a verse right out of its context regardless of the speaker and say, "There, God said that." However, God said nothing of the kind. God's Word says that the devil said it or a bad man said it or a good man said it or an inspired man said it, or an uninspired man said it, or an angel said it. What God says is true, namely, that the devil said it, or a bad man, or a good man, or an inspired man, or an uninspired man, or an angel. However, what they said may or may not be true.

It is very common to hear men quote what Eliphaz, Bildad or Zophar said to Job as if it were necessarily God's own words because it is recorded in the Bible, in spite of the fact that God disavowed their teaching and said to them, "you have not spoken of me what is right" (Job 42:7). It is true that these men said the thing that God records them as saying, but often they gave the truth a twist and said what is not right. A very large share of our difficulties thus arises from not noticing who is speaking. The Bible always tells us, and we should always note it. Below, under the subheadings of "the Case of Job" and "The Comforters" Andrews demonstrates how the erroneous interpretations come about.

The Case of Job

What we have covered thus far will help us understand one of the more complex books of the Bible, the book of Job.

Job was a "blameless and upright man, who fears God and turns away from evil." Job was living the happy life; he had seven sons and the daughters. He was a wealthy landowner. "He possessed 7,000 sheep, 3,000 camels, 500 yoke of oxen, and 500 female donkeys, and very many servants, so that this man was the greatest of all the people of the east." (1:3) Even so, he is not a materialistic person; he was simply following a proverb like the above, 'if you work hard, your efforts will be blessed.'

Job 1:13-19; 2:7-8 English Standard Version (ESV)

[13]Now there was a day when his sons and daughters were eating and drinking wine in their oldest brother's house, [14]and there came a messenger to Job and said, "The oxen were plowing and the donkeys feeding beside them, [15]and the Sabeans fell upon them and took them and struck down the servants with the edge of the sword, and I alone have escaped to tell you." [16]While he was yet speaking, there came another and said, "The fire of God fell from heaven and burned up the sheep and the servants and consumed them, and I alone have escaped to tell you." [17]While he was yet speaking, there came another and said, "The Chaldeans formed three groups and made a raid on the camels and took them and struck down the servants with the edge of the sword, and I alone have escaped to tell you." [18]While he was yet speaking, there came another and said, "Your sons and daughters were eating and drinking wine in their oldest brother's house, [19]and behold, a great wind came across the wilderness and struck the four corners of the house, and it fell upon the young people, and they are dead, and I alone have escaped to tell you." [2:7]So Satan went out from the presence of the LORD and struck Job with loathsome sores from the sole of his foot to the crown of his head. [8]And he took a piece of broken pottery with which to scrape himself while he sat in the ashes.

The Comforters

Job 4:7-8 English Standard Version (ESV)

[7]"Remember: who that was innocent ever perished? Or where were the upright cut off? [8]As I have seen, those who plow iniquity and sow trouble reap the same.

Eliphaz in an attempt at dealing with Job's atrocities assumes Job's tragedies are a result of his own actions. Eliphaz has reasoned wrong by taking a proverb and making it an absolute. In essence, he asks Job, 'do those that are innocent die? When have those that live a righteous life been destroyed?' Eliphaz goes on by saying, 'my experience suggests that it is those who are doing wrong and entertain bad that will get back what they gave out.' In other words, Eliphaz is assuming that only the wicked reap bad times.

Job 5:15 English Standard Version (ESV)

[15]But he saves the needy from the sword of their mouth and from the hand of the mighty.

Eliphaz again assumes that Job is at fault. Eliphaz is assuming that it was Job's great riches, which were ill gotten, and this is why he is suffering. Is Eliphaz's statement wrong in and of itself? No, God does rescue the poor from the oppressive, by their following his counsel on the right way to live. However, this is no absolute; saying all who live by God's will and purposes will never be mistreated. Moreover, the whole idea is misplaced, in that maybe Job is the rich oppressor and this is his punishment from God.

Job 8:3-6 English Standard Version (ESV)

[3]Does God pervert justice? Or does the Almighty pervert the right? [4]If your children have sinned against him, he has delivered them into the hand of their transgression.[5]If you will seek God and plead with the Almighty for mercy, [6]if you are pure and upright, surely then he will rouse himself for you and restore your rightful habitation.

Bildad too is stating true statements, but in absolute terms that are misplaced when it comes to Job, or anyone. Certainly, God does not pervert justice. Therefore, Bildad is right on that, but his application and understanding is what is twisted, as he assumes that children died because they had sinned, and justice was being meted out to them. Again, in verse 5-6, we have a true thought, in that if one is in an impure state, and turns to God with pleadings, he will restore them. However, in verses 5-6, Bildad is assuming that Job is unrighteous, because he sees that proverb as an absolute.

As can be seen from the above, one must be aware that proverbs are not absolutes, but are general truths. True enough, there are likely a couple of exceptions to this rule, but that would not negate this rule, and approach of correct interpretation of proverbs.

In the Psalms, we have sometimes, what God said to man and that is always true; but on the other hand, we often have what man said to God, and that may or may not be true. Sometimes, and far oftener than most of us see, it is the voice of the speaker's personal vengeance or despair. This vengeance may be and often is prophetic, but it may be the wronged man committing his cause to Him to whom vengeance belongs (Romans 12:19), and we are not obliged to defend all that he said. In the Psalms, we have even a record of what the fool said, "There is no God" (Psalm 14:1). Now it is true that the fool said it, but the fool lied when he said it. It is God's Word that the fool said it, but what God reports the fool as saying is not God's own word at all but the fool's own word.

Therefore, in studying our Bible, if God is the speaker we must believe what He says. If an inspired man is the speaker, we must believe what he says. If an uninspired man is the speaker, we must judge for ourselves, it is perhaps true, perhaps false. If it is the devil who is speaking, we do well to remember that he was a liar from the beginning; but even the devil may tell the truth sometimes.

The Language in Which the Bible was Written

The Bible is a book of all ages and for all kinds of people, and therefore it was written in the language that continues the same and is understood by all, the language of the common people and of appearances. It was not written in the terminology of science.

Thus, for example, what occurred at the Battle of Gibeon (Joshua 10:12–14) was described in the way it appeared to those who saw it, and the way in which it would be understood by those who read about it. There is no talk about the refraction of the sun's rays, and so forth, but the sun is said to have "*stood still*" (or tarried) in the midst of heaven. It is one of the perfections of the Bible that it was not written in the terminology of modern science. If it had been, it would never have been understood until the present day, and even now it would be understood only by a few. Furthermore, as science and its terminology are constantly changing, the Bible if written in the terminology of the science of today would be out of date in a few years; but being written in just the language chosen, it has proved the Book for all ages, all lands and all conditions of men.

Other difficulties from the language in which the Bible was written arise from the fact that large portions of the Bible are poetical and are written in the language of poetry, the language of feeling, passion, imagination and figure. Now if a man is hopelessly matter-of-fact, he will inevitably find difficulties with these poetical portions of the inspired Word.

For example, in Psalm 18 we have a marvelous description of a thunderstorm, but let the dull, matter-of-fact fellow get hold of that, for example, verse 8: "Smoke went up from his nostrils, and devouring fire from his mouth; glowing coals flamed forth from him," and he will be head over heels in difficulty at once. However, the trouble is not with the Bible, but with his own stupid, thickheaded plainness.

Our Defective Knowledge of the History, Geography and Usages of Bible Times

For example, in Acts 13:7 Luke speaks of "the deputy" (more accurately "the proconsul," see English Standard Version) of Cyprus. Roman provinces were of two classes, imperial and senatorial. The ruler of the imperial provinces was called a propraetor, of a senatorial province a proconsul. Up to a comparatively recent date, according to the best information we had, Cyprus was an imperial province and therefore its ruler would be a propraetor, but Luke calls him a proconsul. This certainly seemed like a clear case of error on Luke's part, and even the conservative commentators felt forced to admit that Luke was in slight error, and the destructive critics were delighted to find this "mistake." Further and more thorough investigation has brought to light the fact that just at the time of which Luke wrote the senate had made an exchange with the emperor whereby Cyprus had become a senatorial province, and therefore its ruler was a proconsul. Luke was right after all, and the literary critics were themselves in error.

Repeatedly further researches and discoveries, geographical, historical and archaeological, have vindicated the Bible and put to shame its critics. For example, the book of Daniel has naturally been one of the books that unbelievers and destructive critics have most hated. One of their strongest arguments against its authenticity and truthfulness was that such a person as Belshazzar was unknown to history, that all historians agreed that Nabonidus was the last king of Babylon, and that he was absent from the city when it was captured. Therefore, Belshazzar must be a purely mythical character, and the whole story legendary and not historical. Their argument seemed very strong. In fact, it seemed unanswerable. However, Sir H. Rawlinson discovered at Mugheir and other Chaldean sites clay cylinders on which Belshazzar (Belsaruzar) is named by Nabonidus as his eldest son. Doubtless he reigned as regent in the city during his father's absence, an indication of which we have in his proposal to make Daniel third ruler in the kingdom (Daniel 5:16). He himself being second ruler in the kingdom, Daniel would be next to him. So the Bible was vindicated again.

The critics asserted most positively that Moses could not have written the Pentateuch because writing was unknown in his day. However, recent discoveries have proved beyond a question that writing far antedates the time of Moses. So the critics have been compelled to give up their argument, though they have had the bad grace to hold on stubbornly to their conclusion.

The Ignorance of Conditions under Which Books Were Written and Commands Given

For example, to one ignorant of the conditions, God's commands to Israel as to the extermination of the Canaanites seem cruel and horrible. However, when one understands the moral condition to which these nations had sunk, the utter hopelessness of reclaiming them and the weakness of the Israelites themselves, their extermination seems to have been an act of mercy to all succeeding generations and to themselves.

The Many-Sidedness of the Bible

The broadest-minded man is one-sided, but the truth is many-sided, and the Bible is all-sided. Therefore, to our narrow thought one part of the Bible seems to contradict another.

For example, religious men as a rule are either Calvinistic or Arminian in their mental makeup. In addition, some portions of the Bible are decidedly Calvinistic and present great difficulties to the Arminian type of mind, while other portions are decidedly Arminian and present difficulties to the Calvinistic type of mind. However, both sides are true.

Many men in our day are broad-minded enough to be able to grasp at the same time the Calvinistic side of the truth and the Arminian side of the truth; but some are not, so the Bible perplexes, puzzles and bewilders them. The trouble is not with the Bible, but with their own lack of capacity for comprehensive thought.

Expansion: These schools of doctrinal positions are initially established religious leaders and their followers, such as John Calvin and Jacob Arminius. There are even more, such as the Lutheran, from Martin Luther, The Wesleyan, from John Wesley, and the Mennonites, from Menno Simons, and Society of Friends (Quakers) under George Fox. Actually, I would disagree with Torrey here, I believe that he should have used his earlier point of argument, it boils down to the truth of the Bible as being absolute, but man may misinterpret that truth. Therefore, it will lay concealed until discovered. This misinterpretation does not refute the infallibility or inerrancy of Scripture. Actually, doctrine plays no part in inerrancy of Scripture. Whether one believes the earth was created in six literal 24-hour days, or six creative periods called days, has no impact on the doctrine of inerrancy. The Bible is inerrant and one of those interpretations is wrong and the other is correct. This has to do with the person interpreting the Bible, not the inerrancy of the Bible. **Edward D. Andrews**

Therefore, Paul seems to contradict James, and James seems sometimes to contradict Paul; and what Paul says in one place seems to contradict what he says in another place. However, the whole trouble is that our narrow minds cannot take in God's large truth.

The Bible has to do with the Infinite, and our Minds are Finite

It is necessarily difficult to put the facts of infinite being into the limited capacity of our finite intelligence, just as it is difficult to put the ocean into a pint cup. To this class of difficulties belong those connected with the Bible doctrines of the Trinity and of the divine-human nature of Christ. To those who forget that God is infinite, the doctrine of the Trinity seems like the mathematical monstrosity of making one equal three. However, when one bears in mind that the doctrine of the Trinity is an attempt to put into forms of finite thought the facts of infinite being, and into material forms of expression the facts of the spirit, the difficulties vanish. The simplicity of the Unitarian conception of God arises from its shallowness.

The Dullness of our Spiritual Perception

The man who is farthest advanced spiritually is still so immature that he cannot expect to see everything yet as an absolutely holy God sees it, unless he takes it upon simple faith in Him. To this class of difficulties belong those connected with the Bible doctrine of eternal punishment. It often seems to us as if this doctrine cannot be true, must not be true, but the whole difficulty arises from the fact that we are still so blind spiritually that we have no adequate conception of the awfulness of sin, and especially of the awfulness of the sin of rejecting the infinitely glorious Son of God. However, when we become so holy, so like God, that we see the enormity of sin as He sees it, we shall have no difficulty with the doctrine of eternal punishment.

Expansion: Torrey is like many other Calvinist or Lutheran minded individuals, he wishes to follow the evidence, but instead, desires to call those, who do not find this doctrine Biblical, spiritually blind. I hope that even the most conservative reader can see that as dismissive. Without arguing the evidence, I will say that once again, the truth is biblical, and we must follow it objectively, and not allow theological bias to cloud our judgment. I am recommending that you read the following articles.[103]
Edward D. Andrews

As we look back over the ten classes of difficulties, we see they all arise from our imperfection, and not from the imperfection of the Bible. The Bible is perfect, but we, being imperfect, have difficulty with it. As we grow more and more into the perfection of God, our difficulties grow ever less and less, and so we are forced to conclude that when we become as perfect as God is, we shall have no more difficulties whatever with the Bible.

---

[103] **Hellfire - Eternal Torment?**

http://www.christianpublishers.org/hellfire-eternal-torment
Hellfire - Is It Just?

http://www.christianpublishers.org/hellfire-is-it-just

Review Question

- Explain some of the different types of Bible difficulties?

Other Books By Edward D. Andrews

WHO IS THE ANTICHRIST

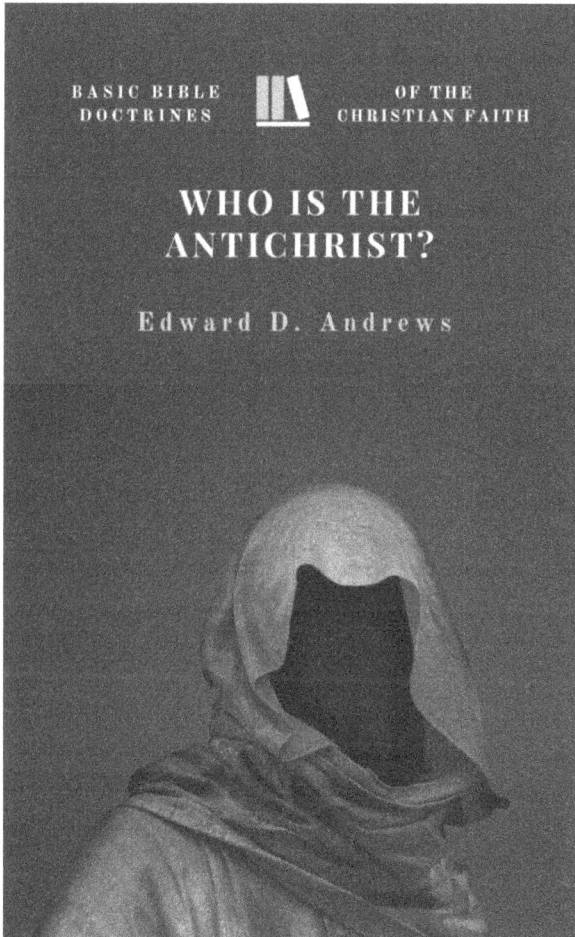

What Is Hell?

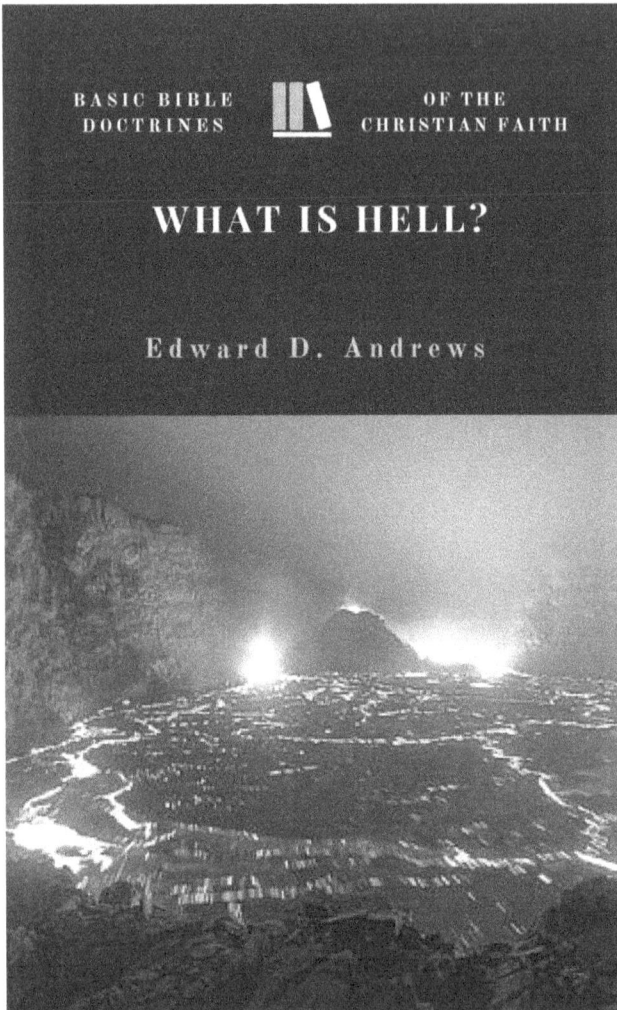

BASIC BIBLE
DOCTRINES

OF THE
CHRISTIAN FAITH

WHAT IS HELL?

Edward D. Andrews

The SECOND COMING of CHRIST

BASIC BIBLE DOCTRINES OF THE CHRISTIAN FAITH

The SECOND COMING of CHRIST

Edward D. Andrews

Where Are the Dead?

Explaining the Holy Spirit

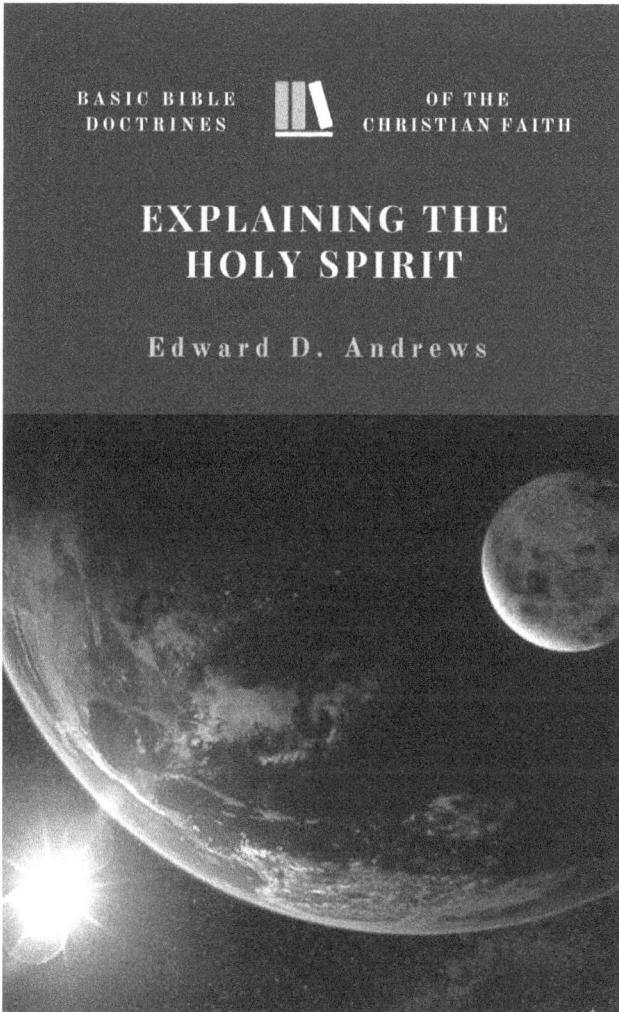

BASIC BIBLE
DOCTRINES

OF THE
CHRISTIAN FAITH

EXPLAINING THE HOLY SPIRIT

Edward D. Andrews

BASIC BIBLE DOCTRINES   OF THE CHRISTIAN FAITH

EXPLAINING THE DOCTRINE OF SALVATION

Edward D. Andrews

Bibliography

Archer, Gleason L. *Encyclopedia of Bible Difficulties.* Grand Rapids: Zondervan, 1982.

Balz, Horst, and Gerhard Schneider. *Exegetical Dictionary of the New Testament.* Edinburgh: T & T Clark Ltd, 1978.

Bercot, David W. *A Dictionary of Early Christian Beliefs.* Peabody: Hendrickson, 1998.

Brand, Chad, Charles Draper, and England Archie. *Holman Illustrated Bible Dictionary: Revised, Updated and Expanded.* Nashville, TN: Holman, 2003.

Bromiley, Geoffrey W. *The International Standard Bible Encyclopedia (Vol. 1-4).* Grand Rapids, MI: William B. Eerdmans Publishing Co., 1986.

Bromiley, Geoffrey W., and Gerhard Friedrich. *Theological Dictionary of the New Testament, ed. Gerhard Kittel, vol. 4.* Grand Rapids, MI: Eerdmans, 1964-.

Collins, John. *Genesis 1-4: A Linguistic, Literary, and Theological Commentary.* Philipsburg: P&R, 2006.

Cornwall, Judson, and Stelman Smith. *The Exhaustive Dictionary of Bible Names.* Gainsville: Bridge-Logos, 1998.

Davis, John J. *Paradise to Prison: Studies in Genesis.* Salem: Sheffield, 1975.

Elwell, Walter A. *Baker Encyclopedia of the Bible.* Grand Rapids: Baker Book House, 1988.

—. *Evangelical Dictionary of Theology (Second Edition).* Grand Rapids: Baker Academic, 2001.

Elwell, Walter A, and Philip Wesley Comfort. *Tyndale Bible Dictionary.* Wheaton, III: Tyndale House Publishers, 2001.

Garrett, Duane. *Rethinking Genesis: The Sources and Authorship of the First Book of the Pentateuch .* Grand Rapids: Baker Books, 1991.

Geisler, Norman L., and Thomas Howe. *The Big Book of Bible Difficulties.* Grand Rapids: Baker Books, 1992.

Green, Joel B, Scot McKnight, and Howard Marshall. *Dictionary of Jesus and the Gospels.* Downers Grove, IL: InterVarsity Press, 1992.

Gunkel, Hermann. *The Stories of Genesis. Translated by John J. Scullion. Edited by William R. Scott.* Berkeley: BIBAL, 1994.

Hastings, James, John A Selbie, and John C Lambert. *A Dictionary of Christ and the Gospels.* New York, NY: Charles Scribner's Sons, 1907.

Hindson, Ed, and Ergun Caner. *The Popular Encyclopedia of Apologetics: Surveying the Evidence for the Truth of Christianity.* Eugene: Harvest House, 2008.

Kissling, Paul J. *The College Press NIV commentary: Genesis.* Joplin, MO: College Press Pub. Co., 2004.

Language, John Peter. *A Commentary on the Holy Scriptures: Genesis.* Bellingham: Logos Research Systems, 1939, 2008.

Mathews, K. A. *The New American Commentary vol. 1A, Genesis 1-11:26 .* Nashville: Broadman & Holman Publishers, 2001.

Matthews, K. A. *The New American Commentary Vol. 1B, Genesis 11:27-50:26.* Nashville: Broadman and Holman Publishers, 2001.

Mirriam-Webster, Inc. *Mirriam-Webster's Collegiate Dictionary. Eleventh Edition.* Springfield: Mirriam-Webster, Inc., 2003.

Morris, Henry M. *The Genesis Record: A Scientific and Devotional Commentary on the Book of the Beginnings.* Grand Rapids: Baker Books, 2007, 1976.

Mounce, William D. *Mounce's Complete Expository Dictionary of Old & New Testament Words.* Grand Rapids, MI: Zondervan, 2006.

Myers, Allen C. *The Eerdmans Bible Dictionary .* Grand Rapids, Mich: Eerdmans, 1987.

Reyburn, William David, and Euan Mc G. Fry. *A Handbook on Genesis (UBS Handbook Series).* New York: United Bible Societies, 1997.

Swanson, James. *A Dictionary of Biblical Languages - Greek.* Washington: Logos Research Systems, 1997.

Vine, W E. *Vine's Expository Dictionary of Old and New Testament Words.* Nashville: Thomas Nelson, 1996.

Walton, John H. *Zondervan Illustrated Bible Backgrounds Commentary (Old Testament) Volume 1: Genesis, Exodus, Leviticus, Numbers, Deuteronomy.* Grand Rapids, MI: Zondervan, 2009.

Walton, John H. *THE NIV APPLICATION COMMENTARY Genesis.* Grand Rapids: Zondervan, 2001.

Wood, D R W. *New Bible Dictionary (Third Edition).* Downers Grove: InterVarsity Press, 1996.

Zodhiates, Spiros. *The Complete Word Study Dictionary: New Testament.* Chattanooga: AMG Publishers, 2000, c1992, c1993.

www.ingramcontent.com/pod-product-compliance
Lightning Source LLC
Chambersburg PA
CBHW031959040426
42448CB00006B/419